Excerpts from

THE GETTING BACK TO NATURE DIET

The high cost of "*convenience living*" is taking its toll on the health of the nation. One day the human body parts business may be bigger than the auto parts enterprises.

chapter 1

* * *

A diet of "*hamburger, french fries and a cola*" is a nutritional Titanic!

chapter 2

* * *

Have you ever been to a hospital lately? There are *right* nostril specialists and *left* nostril specialists. And heaven help you if you get into the wrong room!

chapter 3

* * *

The tale goes on that the priest Imam Bayeldi had a thousand wives. And whenever they served a dinner of Eggplant he swooned with ecstasy!

chapter 4

* * *

One of the basic reasons we cannot cope with today's problems is because of today's diet. Right now we are almost hypnotized for a world leader to come in and take us over to run us like automatons!

chapter 5

* * *

Sometimes we get so mysticized by the mechanics of medicine . . . that we automatically believe that anything that complicated and official looking just has to be good for our physical ailment.

chapter 7

* * *

Nutritionists have found the carrot a most valuable food. They believe the carrot provides energy, combats anemia, promotes normal elimination while preventing diarrhea.

chapter 9

* * *

Has anyone ever erected a statue to the Okra? Why hasn't the President of the United States declared July 5th as National Okra Day?   chapter 12

* * *

If I had to choose between gold and garlic, I'd choose garlic . . . for it is nature's gold!

chapter 13

* * *

What has happened to our lives? Why do we become slaves to a stress environment? This complex civilization confronts us with many more monumental problems than our forefathers faced. Yet, how can we be joyful, when, on the surface, there appears to be nothing to be joyful about?

chapter 16

* * *

How many years have you been blind to supplying your body with the nutritious fuel it requires. There are ten guidelines for a **Back to Nature Diet**.

chapter 18

All this and much more you will find in **THE GETTING BACK TO NATURE DIET**. Practical guidelines for healthy and happy living!

Presented to

_____

By

_____

_____

_____

Date

_____

The Getting Back To Nature Diet

by Salem Kirban

Published by SALEM KIRBAN, Inc., Kent Road, Huntingdon Valley, Pennsylvania, 19006. Copyright © 1978 by Salem Kirban. Printed in the United States of America.

ISBN 0-912582-28-6
Library of Congress Catalog Card No. 78-50018

Eggplant

Celery - Stabilize stomach function
Vit. C, A   Build blood cells
Potassium   Kidney function
Magnesium   Energy
              Anti Arthritic action
              Calm nerves & ease tension
              Diuretic

Yogurt - Relieve Constipation   Lowers Cholesterol
Protein   Indigestion
Calcium
Potassium   Stomach Ulcers
Iron Assimilation   Gallbladder Disease
            Gas
            Colitis
            Cancer

DEDICATION

My wife
MARY

*"Who can find a
virtuous woman?*

*For her price is
far above rubies.*

*A virtuous woman
is a crown to her
husband. . ."*

(Proverbs 31:10; 12:4)

My wife, Mary.
Her life is a constant inspiration to me.

ACKNOWLEDGMENTS

To **Doreen Frick,** who carefully proofread the text.

To **Koechel Designs,** who designed the front cover.

To **William Guerin** and **Duane Kirban** who assisted in the preparation of the Food Values charts.

To **Walter W. Slotilock,** Chapel Hill Litho, for skillfully making the illustration negatives.

To **Batsch Company, Inc.,** for excellent craftsmanship in setting the type quickly.

To **The Printers,** for printing with all possible speed and quality.

To **Aunt Effie,** who contributed her opinions. Everyone has an Aunt Effie who thinks she knows the answer to every problem. You'll enjoy her old fashioned remedies but check them out with your doctor.

Scriptures used include the King James Version of the Bible and The New American Standard Bible (NASV). NASV by permission of the Lockman Foundation.

CONTENTS

NOTE

The author is **not** a medical doctor. Nor is he posing as one! He is an investigative reporter. The author is interested in teaching the health message as found in the Bible.

The author makes no claims for a cure for any disease! Nor do we believe that drugs cure disease. Disease can only be corrected by the body's own healing and health-restoring power through God's grace.

We do not believe that the human body suffers from a deficiency of aspirin or a tranquilizer drug, etc. We do believe that most Americans are overfed and undernourished. We also believe that sound, intelligent nutrition practices are the first defense against disease and a better first alternative.

Nothing in this book, however, should imply to you that following this diet will solve your health problems. Nor do we in any way suggest you should put off seeking proper health advice from your doctor when the need arises.

It does cost money to maintain good health. But it costs much, much more to regain health once you have lost it!

WHY I WROTE THIS BOOK

This week the British Cunard Lines announced the world's most expensive cruise — a 90-day tour of the Pacific for a mere $160,000 first class.

For that price you get the penthouse suite on the Queen Elizabeth, where the railings are gold-plated and the wall panels are handwoven silk. The furniture and service matches and the silver dishes are kept filled with beluga caviar.

No doubt several people will rush to fill this accommodation. I sense that the world has gone pleasure-mad. It's a manufactured joy, which, when the tinseled box is open, reveals nothing but emptiness. There is a tendency to worship film and television stars who dress gaudily and live extravagantly.

We tend to measure a person's success in how much money he has stockpiled or how many homes and cars he owns or whether he has achieved a meteoric rise in business. Unfortunately this yardstick has crept even into the field of religion. Recently "born again" celebrities are rocketed to further prominence on religious TV extravaganzas. **And our children, impressed by this warped sense of reality, tend to strive toward the same goals of worldly success.**

Coupled with this the average child sees between 8500 to 13,000 television food commercials each year. Dr. Jean Mayer, President of Tufts University in Boston states that by the age of 18, children have spent two years watching television. And by the age 60, the average American has been exposed to the equivalent on nine working years of TV viewing. No wonder the ten largest food advertisers spend 90% of their advertising budgets on television.

In one year, children will see some 3300 advertisements for sugary breakfast cereals, 1600 advertisements for candy and 800 for cookies. Whereas they will only see 2 commercials for meat and poultry **and only 1 for vegetables.** Dr. Mayer says this is ". . .*nutrition educating in reverse.*"

Six out of ten of the leading causes of death in the United States have been linked to the way we eat. Over 25 million Americans are diabetic. At least one-fourth of all adults in the United States are overweight!

I think it is time we **GET BACK TO NATURE** . . . get back to the simple things in life our parents knew (and their parents before them). Let's stop measuring success in wealth, in material possessions, in pleasures. **This is the first step to a healthy mind.** And let's stop feeding ourselves, and our children, junk foods and start eating fresh vegetables, wholesome grains and fruit in season. **This is the first step to a healthy body.** It's time for each of us to ask the question: "*Where are we headed?*" And it's time to reassess our priorities in life. That's why I wrote this book!

Salem Kirban

Huntingdon Valley, Pennsylvania
U.S.A., January, 1978

1

THE DAY THE TREES DISAPPEAR

Reaping the Bitter Harvest

Nature, to be commanded, must be obeyed. And, for too long, we have been ignoring the laws of nature. Now, we are reaping the whirlwind of disease and death. We are turning verdant green pastures into giant shopping malls and parking lots. Our country has been criss-crossed with super highways. Soon America may become one solid piece of concrete!

Our factories are working overtime, spewing pollutants out into the atmosphere while endeavoring to meet the insatiable appetite of the consumer. Last year, as an example, consumers spent over $570 million just on deodorants and antiperspirants plus another $300 million on mouthwash.

The Human Parts Business

The high cost of "convenience living" is taking its toll on the health of the nation. And more and more parts in the body, that are beyond repair, are now simply being surgically removed. This has given rise to a new breed of engineer . . . the engineer who specializes in medical equipment and human parts. One day the human body parts business may be bigger than the auto parts enterprises. Doctors now daily implant teflon esophagi, plastic knuckles, plastic kneecaps, plastic hip joints, plastic bones and plastic arteries among a host of other substitutes.

Our Food is Killing Us

Part of the reason for this is that we are eating "plastic" bread and highly processed foods. Food processors are putting sugar in everything from hot dogs and cold cuts to vegetables and salad dressings. It has been said that 90% of the cancers are due to our environment. This is not difficult to understand.

In an article in the July 25, 1977 issue of the Journal of American Medicine, Dr. Theodore C. Bernstein writes:

> At a formal dinner one evening last year, I was seated beside a young woman, a physician, who posed a question because I, an oncologist, should know the answer.
>
> *What are my chances of getting breast cancer? Every woman in my mother's family has breast cancer or has died of it; my mother, her mother, my mother's sister, the sister's daughter, and my own sister. With a family history like that, what are my chances?*

This penetrating question should cause all of us to wake up and show concern about our living patterns. Is it possible that the poor eating habits of past generations could be reflected in diseases in our children's children?

Celery

Warnings: As with most CNS-acting drugs, caution against hazardous occupations requiring complete mental alertness (e.g., operating machinery, driving). Withdrawal symptoms (similar to those with barbiturates, alcohol) have occurred following abrupt discontinuance (convulsions, tremor, abdominal/muscle cramps, vomiting, sweating). Keep addiction-prone individuals (drug addicts or alcoholics) under careful surveillance because of predisposition to habituation/dependence.

Usage in Pregnancy: **Use of minor tranquilizers during first trimester should almost always be avoided because of increased risk of congenital malformations, as suggested in several studies. Consider possibility of pregnancy when instituting therapy; advise patients to discuss therapy if they intend to or do become pregnant.**

ORAL: Advise patients against simultaneous ingestion of alcohol and other CNS depressants.

Not of value in treatment of psychotic patients; should not be emplo~~...~~ appropriate treatment. When using oral form adjunctively in ~~...~~ possibility of increase in frequency and/or severity of ~~...~~ increase in dosage of standard anticonvulsan~~...~~ such cases may be associated with t~~...~~ of seizures.

INJECTABLE: *To reduce t~~...~~ swelling, and. r~~...~~ least on~~...~~*

(overlapping diagonal duplicate text): Warnings: As with most CNS-acting drugs, caution again requiring complete mental alertness (e.g., operating mac symptoms (similar to those with barbiturates, alcohol) ha abrupt discontinuance (convulsions, tremor, abdominal sweating). Keep addiction-prone individuals (drug addic ful surveillance because of predisposition to habituatio

~~...~~ eased risk of ~~...~~ arcotic analgesic ~~...~~ter in small increments. ~~...~~coma, acute alcoholic intoxication ~~...~~cus in patients treated for petit mal status or ~~...~~ (similar to those with barbiturates, alcohol) have occurred ~~...~~ discontinuance (convulsions, tremor, abdominal/muscle cramps, ~~...~~ sweating). Keep addiction-prone individuals under careful surveillance ~~...~~cause of predisposition to habituation/dependence. Not recommended for OB use.

Efficacy/safety not established in neonates (age 30 days or less); prolonged CNS-depression observed. In children, give slowly (up to 0.25 mg/kg over 3 minutes) to avoid apnea or prolonged somnolence; can be repeated after 15 to 30 minutes. If no relief after third administration, appropriate adjunctive therapy is recommended.

Precautions: If combined with other psychotropics or anticonvulsants, carefully consider individual pharmacologic effects—particularly with known compounds which may potentiate action of Valium (diazepam), i.e., phenothiazines, narcotics, barbiturates, MAO inhibitors and antidepressants. Protective measures indicated in highly anxious patients with accompanying depression who may have suicidal tendencies. Observe usual precautions in impaired hepatic function; avoid accumulation in patients with compromised kidney function. Limit oral dosage to smallest effective amount in elderly and debilitated to preclude ataxia or oversedation (initially 2 to 2½ mg once or twice daily, increasing gradually as needed or tolerated). INJECTABLE: Although promptly controlled, seizures may return; readminister if necessary; not recommended for long-term maintenance therapy. Laryngospasm/increased cough reflex are possible during peroral endoscopic procedures; use topical anesthetic, have necessary countermeasures available. Hypotension or muscular weakness possible, particularly when used with narcotics, barbiturates or alcohol. Use lower doses (2 to 5 mg) for elderly/debilitated.

Adverse Reactions: Side effects most commonly reported were drowsiness, fatigue, ataxia. Infrequently encountered were confusion, constipation, depression, diplopia, dysarthria, headache, hypotension, incontinence, jaundice, changes in libido, nausea, changes in salivation, skin rash, slurred speech, tremor, urinary retention, vertigo, blurred vision. Paradoxical reactions such as acute hyper-excited states, anxiety, hallucinations, increased muscle spasticity, insomnia, rage, sleep disturbances and stimulation have been reported; should these occur, discontinue drug. Because of isolated reports of neutropenia and jaundice, periodic blood counts, liver function tests advisable during long-term therapy. Minor changes in EEG patterns, usually low-voltage fast activity, have been observed in patients during and after Valium (diazepam) therapy and are of no known significance.

Adverse Reactions: NONE

Benefits:

Celery contains...

Calcium	Iron
Phosphorus	Sodium
Chlorine	Potassium
Copper	Vitamin A
Iodine	Thiamin
Magnesium	Riboflavin
Manganese	Niacin
Sulfur	
Ascorbic Acid	

Two stalks provide:

1 gram protein

Celery is "nature's Valium."
This is not to infer that Valium is
not sometimes indiciated

Celery is "nature's Valium."
This is not to infer that Valium
is not sometimes indicated in
selected circumstances. But
rather to point out the widespread
misuse of drug tranquilizers;
a misuse even recognized by
responsible medical doctors!

On the left are the side effects of Valium as listed in standard medical journals. Inset shows actual size of type face which is 6 pt. or 1/16″ of an inch high. Most drugs list side effects this long and even longer . . . always in small, difficult to read type. Even trained physicians find it impossible to keep abreast of new drugs and their multiplicity of side effects. Is it any wonder the patient is confused and tends to look upon his doctor as a god?

When we become ill (with some exceptions) our body is suffering from a lack of proper nutrition . . . improper fueling and constant abuse. Should not nutrition be the *first* alternative against disease?

**Inheriting
the Sins of
Our Fathers**

We call this a disease because of heredity. But do these diseases occur because the children adapt the same poor eating and living habits? It is interesting to note what the Bible says in several places including in the Old Testament book of Numbers:

> The Lord is slow to anger and abundant in loving kindness, forgiving iniquity and transgression; but He will by no means clear the guilty, visiting the iniquity of the fathers on the children to the third and the fourth generations.
>
> (Numbers 14:18 NAS)

When parents ill-treat their body by eating foods that harm their body, they are showing disrespect for the temple of the Holy Spirit. See 1 Corinthians 6:19-20. The habits that the parents have are most often then passed on to their children and then to their children's children. Understanding this, we can better understand Numbers 14:18 which reveals that the sins of the fathers are passed on even to the 4th generation.

Is it no wonder that the young woman physician was concerned that she might develop breast cancer? Now, of course, this is too simple an explanation and I am sure some physician will say breast cancer susceptibility is indicated by:

> Cyclic ovarian activity reflected by menarche (onset of menses), age of first pregnancy, marriage state, overweight women and chronic cystic mastitis.

But in my own simple (and certainly unscientific analysis) I would tend to believe that most cancer is caused by the environment in which we live. This environment may be in the form of not only the pollutants that have invaded every facet of our lives, but in the eating sins that have been passed down to us through our parents.

Too Much Knowledge

I believe there is a dangerous trend to try to explain everything scientifically. Some doctors (not all) tend to look down their noses at the suggestion that eating proper foods can keep a person well or make him better. This appears to them to be too simplistic. They have been schooled in the art of prescribing a drug for every ailment and if that doesn't work to cut out the ailing part. Nutrition is rarely the first alternative. In fact, the patient who is tense or nervous (with no specific ailment) would be shocked if the doctor handed him a stalk of celery to chew on instead of Valium. That doctor would be considered a "quack."

And Not Enough Common Sense

From a scientific viewpoint it is impossible, by the standards of aerodynamics, for a bee to be able to fly. But he does . . . in spite of science! The world is full of seeming impossibilities.

Yet, because we cannot fathom the full depth of them, this does not make them untrue!

The science of nutrition is the science of nature. There are certain laws that must be obeyed.

One law reminds us that there are basic nutrients required by every living cell if we expect to remain alive and well.

Another law indicates that wastes must be eliminated.

The basic nutrients our body requires include protein, minerals, vitamins, fatty acids and glucose.

Colon Clogging Diets

A diet which consists mainly of highly processed foods, hamburgers on soggy, colon-clogging buns, french fries, sugary cakes, pies, ice cream and candy is not conducive to keeping our body alive and well. Nor does it help us in daily eliminating wastes from our system.

No reasonable man would put water in his gas tank. Yet that same individual will think nothing of polluting his body with wrong foods plus alcohol, nicotine and caffeine.

It was sad to watch an annual Athletes' Award dinner on television recently where most of the principal characters were smoking big cigars and sipping on cocktails.

The End of the Road

One TV commentary included an interview with a woman who had smoked a pack of cigarettes a day for some 20 years. She said she took up smoking because the ads told her it would give her prestige and make her sexy. The TV camera zoomed in on her face. Now in her early 40's, she was haggard and wrinkled. Her head was covered with a bonnet. She had been through the route of chemotherapy and her hair had fallen out. She was dying of lung cancer and she moaned: *"It just isn't fair. Here I am at the prime of my life when I should be living and enjoying life. But I'm at the end of the road and it isn't sexy."*

She died just 6 days later.

The sins of the fathers will reach down to the third and fourth generation!

Isn't it about time we woke up?

Should we all take a moment to pause and ask ourselves the question:

What direction are we going?

Our Values Are Warped

We are headed towards an artificial, plastic world that offers us:

> A credit card . . . without the need of money. Miracle drugs . . . without concern for the side effects. More convenience foods . . . without the necessary nutrients. Bigger cars . . . without concern for the quality of our air. Faster planes . . . without concern for our atmosphere. More manufactured foods . . . without concern for our waterways. Cattle that are chemical food machines . . . without concern for our health.

As a result of this maddening race for disaster, we are the world leader in deaths caused by heart disease. The number of patients admitted to hospitals is increasing at a rate five times faster than the growth of our population. Breast cancer is developing in one woman out of every 15. One family in seven has a member who undergoes surgery in any given year.

We give a candy bar as a reward for good behavior, we pack lunch boxes with cupcakes instead of apples after starting our

Nature has taken a back seat for "progress." Many believe a pill will solve every ill. As our sophisticated diets are destroying our health . . . so our drive for materialism is destroying our natural resources. It is not inconceivable that one day we may walk into a museum to see a LIVING TREE EXHIBIT.

youngsters off with a sugared breakfast cereal and a synthetic orange juice made with a powder mix.

Nature is a volume of which God is the author.

And it's about time we start getting back to nature and reading her Book!

A University in Which Everyone Should Be a Student

Let us permit nature to have her way: she understands her business better than we do. Let us set aside high and mighty degrees of learning and enroll in the University of Nature.

Over 10 years ago I wrote a novel entitled **666** which had as its setting the year 2000.[1] Because of our irresponsible living habits all the trees in the world had disappeared . . . all, except a few precious trees. These were housed in an exhibit called **THE LIVING TREE** exhibit. It drew the crowds as parents brought their children to the exhibit hall to stand in awe of a real, live, green tree!

I wrote the book as fiction. But they say that truth is stranger than fiction. And this sad revelation may, in years to come, become truth! There may well be a day when the trees disappear.

That's why I wrote this book. It is about time we get back to nature . . . in all ways. For if we are to benefit by its bounty, we must obey its laws.

THE GETTING BACK TO NATURE DIET, I believe, is the first step back that will enable us to move forward. Will you join me in this new adventure?

---

[1] Salem Kirban, **666**, (Kent Road, Huntingdon Valley, Penna. 19006), $2.95.

2

PLEASE PASS THE SAWDUST

**We Live
in a
Garbage
Environment**

Christopher Columbus didn't know where he was going. When he got there he didn't know where he was. And when he got back, he didn't know where he had been! He <u>must</u> have been confused.

But certainly no more confused than most people are today. Our abilities to cope in this world have been weakened catastrophically by the garbage that we put into our bodies and the garbage on television that is fed into our minds.

There is an old computer saying:

*If you put garbage into the
computer . . .
You will get garbage OUT!*

How true! If you program a computer with wrong data . . . it will turn around and promptly feed you back wrong data.

What can we expect of our children when we daily feed them wrong foods and allow them to watch television programming loaded with crime and sex? You can expect GARBAGE!

**Degrees
Without
Intelligence**

This is rather plain English and very pointed. But it is time we wake up to the facts. There is a little poem which reveals:

> My daughter has her Master's
> My son, his Ph.D.
> But father is the only one
> Who has a J-O-B.

After giving our youngsters a daily diet of plastic foods, we badger them to make a name for themselves in life and get a degree. But the world is so overloaded with highly educated young people with degrees that they can't find jobs.

The Getting Back to Nature Diet suggests we slacken the race for more and more head knowledge until we can balance it with a knowledge of the laws of nature which include the laws of sound nutrition.

Our children deserve a fair chance. Why send them out into the race of life with one leg, nutritionally speaking?

**Illness
Begins at
Breakfast**

We start at breakfast time with cereals loaded with sugar, BHT and BHA. Look at the ingredients listed on the box of breakfast cereal you buy. They are listed in the order in which the greatest quantity appears. Thus the first item listed is the item of the greatest quantity in that box or can, etc.

Most breakfast cereals list sugar or malt syrup as their second ingredient. Sugar is sweet suicide! Americans consume on the average of 130 pounds of sugar a year! This averages out to 31 teaspoons of sugar per day. This may

When bran became popular, even the big-name cereal companies jumped on the bandwagon. However, commercial bran cereals have some type of sweetener added. Reading left to right, here is the sugar content of the cereals above: Raisin Bran (10.6), All-Bran (20.0), 100% Bran (18.4), Bran Buds (30.2) and Cracklin' bran.

be hard to visualize but it's true.

**Our
Sugar
Coated
World**

If one's breakfast includes: cereal, waffles or pancakes, muffins with jelly and coffee or tea . . . we have already consumed some 10 teaspoons of sugar. A mid-morning snack with a doughnut or coffee cake adds another 6 teaspoons of sugar. A mid morning snack with a cold-cut sandwich, pie and beverage can total 8 more teaspoons of sugar. Then a soft drink or candy bar in midafternoon adds 6 more teaspoons of sugar. At dinner time we can generally add up 14 more teaspoons of sugar.

Sugar has been promoted as "quick energy." And it does give you energy quickly. And just as quickly it abandons you like a sinking ship and leaves you with fatigue, irritability and a headache. Hypoglycemics understand this cycle full well.

**The
Silent Enemy
That Kills
Sweetly**

What sugar does is throw a monkey wrench into the body's metabolism. It throws the body off balance by providing cells with energy but not feeding them with the nutrients required for them to function properly. It's like giving your son a checkbook to write checks on but not putting any money into that account. Soon, there is a sad awakening.

Sugar is a hollow food. You ingest sugar into your body. To digest this sugar the body has to rob precious nutrients from healthy cells. Sugar is in effect, a freeloader. It contributes nothing to your body but it extracts nutrients and at the same time destroys the B vitamins. Have you ever noticed yourself becoming sleepy after eating a sugar food?

The Hidden Persuader

We think of sugar just being in our breakfast cereals, and ice cream, pies and candy. But food processors are putting sugar in almost everything! Sugar is in hot dogs, in cold cuts, in canned vegetables, in salad dressings, in yogurt, in Stove-Top type stuffing mixes . . . even in Quaker 100% Natural Cereal!

Sugar is the major culprit for diabetes and hypoglycemia and is a contributory cause to vascular diseases, coronary thrombosis, health problems connected with the eyes, the teeth, the skin and joints plus even cancer!

Now I may have digressed here, but it was necessary to convey a very important point.

We start off our day with a breakfast cereal and perhaps pancakes and syrup. And immediately we have started the process of killing our body . . . this time with sugar! Now, at the time, the eating of these foods will tickle our tastebuds. And you may not suffer the consequences of these bad habits until 20 or 30 years from now. But then nature will rebel in full fury!

Sawdust Sandwiches

Lunch usually consists of a sandwich made from white bread and cold cuts. It was Dr. Roger Williams, an eminent biochemist, who said:

> . . . today's bread has about the same nutritional value as sawdust.

Our flour is bleached to death with deadly chemicals which have been approved for use. And as much as 90 preservatives and additives may be added to a loaf of bread without being mentioned on the label! Some people buy wheat bread thinking they are getting a more nutritious value. But look on the label! Most wheat bread is made by mostly white flour! Why housewives judge the worth of bread on whether it is soft is beyond me! If they could only visualize this mass of almost impenetrable dough trying to gain passage through their colon!

The Cold Facts of Cold Cuts

The cold cuts are loaded with nitrites and nitrates. Both sodium nitrite and sodium nitrate are used extensively in the curing process of meats and also of fish. And although the Food and Drug Administration may approve of their use it does not mean they are safe. It is the judgment of many that these additives directly contribute to the higher incidence of cancer.

Our meat, whether it is steak or cold cuts, starts with the many "animal factories" located throughout the country. In their book, How to Get Rid of the Poisons in Your Body,[1] Gary and Steven Null report:

> The animals are kept alive and fattened by the continuous administration of tranquilizers, hormones, antibiotics, and 2700 other F.D.A.-approved drugs. The process starts even before birth and continues long after death.

Cattle are kept on special feedlots where bright sodium-arc lamps are turned on at night. The purpose to make the animal believe it is daylight so that they eat 24 hours a day. With so many injections like DES (to

---

[1] Gary Null and Steven Null, How To Get Rid Of The Poisons In Your Body (New York: Arco Publishing Company, Inc.), 1977, p. 52.

How quickly we slide from the wholesome springtime health of our youth to the overwhelming stress and sickness that often occurs long before the autumn and winter of our adult life! Are we not reaping the bitter harvest that was sown through the years by poor nutrition?

make them grow fatter on less feed) and MGA (to eliminate their sex drive) and tranquilizers to hypnotize them into simply eating without becoming restless . . . it is no wonder they are called "chemical food machines."

Synthetic Steak

Where do all these 2700-some-odd drugs go when the livestock is butchered? Do they just ride off into the sunset?

You can believe that if you wish . . . but the laws of nature cannot be altered. Remember, if you put garbage into the computer . . . you get garbage out of the computer.

And what you put into the livestock . . . will eventually show up on your kitchen table. And if you eat it . . . it will reap its bitter harvest in ensuing years as you start to make trips to the doctor for "unexplained ailments."

The Bargain That is No Bargain

Well, we have had our lunch. And now it is time to turn to dinner. And the easiest way out is to patronize one of the many fast-food-fare restaurants. And we add our few dollars to this almost $15 billion industry!

One of the top fast-food-fare restaurants, had $2,730 MILLIONS of dollars in sales in the U.S. alone in 1976. And this was an increase of 21% over 1975. This type of increase is typical of their competitors as well.

The major problem to the consumer is not the use of these restaurants but, rather, the misuse. More than one out of three meals is now eaten outside the home. This type of continual eating contributes to a deficient diet. One may feel a "hunger satisfaction" when eating there but it is a false security. The total caloric count of a fast-food meal which includes: a full-size hamburger, a milk shake and french fries is 1300 calories. This is 1/2 the daily requirement of an adult male. And this is only one meal. Such continuous eating can contribute to overweight.

The Nutritional Titanic

Not only that, but such a diet of "Hamburger, french fries and coke" is a nutritional Titanic! The hamburger bun has sugar added to it. It becomes soggy and a real colon-clogger, providing no roughage but rather a "stopper." The hamburger contains an average of 20% fat. The french fries are loaded with salt (an excellent contributor to high blood pressure). The soft drink is loaded with sugar and caffeine. The milk shake is high in sugar, has preservatives, emulsifiers and stabilizing agents. Is this what your body needs?

No wonder our youngsters are either hyperactive or suffer from a lack of drive and purpose. You can't put water into a gas tank and expect to have a smooth running car!

And then there is that evening bedtime snack, ice cream! Good old ice cream, *the garbage dump food*" is what Gaye D. Horsley calls it in her book, Commercial Foods Exposed.[1] It is a real chemical cocktail!

It has been reported that some breads are appearing on the market that contain wood chips or sawdust.

This reminds me of the farmer who was rather tight with the dollar. One day, in order to save on feed, he slipped some sawdust in with the

---

[1] Gaye D. Horsley, Commercial Foods Exposed (Salt Lake City: Hawkes Publishing Inc.), 1975, p. 76.

feed that his cattle were eating.

They never knew the difference.

**You Cannot
Fool Nature**

Still anxious to save more money, he got to the point where he would tiptoe into the barn at night, when the cows were asleep and he increased their dose of sawdust ... when they weren't looking.

The next morning the cows continued to eat the "food" that was placed before them.

The farmer was elated!

Finally he got the cows to a point where they were eating a 100% sawdust diet. And the sawdust didn't cost him a penny. He got it from the local lumber mill, free!

The cows never knew the difference!

He was thrilled with his new discovery, so thrilled that one morning he raced over to Farmer Brown's house to tell him of this ingenious savings. Farmer Brown would not believe him. Together they walked over to the barn. True enough, there were the feed bins filled high with sawdust.

And there was every cow ... dead!

How many of us are feeding ourselves and our children on the sawdust of life. We are thrilled. It is cheap. It is satisfying to the appetite. It is quick.

If you continue to flaunt the laws of nature in regards to nutrition, may I suggest 5, 10, 15 years from now, as you sit dejectedly in the doctor's office, you pick up his Gideon Bible and read Numbers 32:23 in the Old Testament which, although out of context, reminds us:

... be sure your sin will find you out!

3

HOW TO LAUGH YOUR WAY BACK TO BETTER HEALTH

**How to
Put Joy
Into Living**

The Bible says:

*A merry heart doeth good like a
medicine . . .*

(Proverbs 17:22 KJV)

A merry heart is a *joyful* heart. What is joy?
Joy is from the word to rejoice. It infers happiness and delight.

I must admit it is sometimes hard to be joyful.
Like right now, as an example. I am seated at
this typewriter at 11 in the morning. It is a hot
August day. Our central air conditioner is
broken. And the Sears service center says
they will be around to fix it in 10 days. It is
cloudy and getting hot and sticky. And this is
the first chapter I am writing of my new book,
The Getting Back to Nature Diet. And I am not
necessarily inspired. Writing is 99% perspiration and 1% inspiration, anyway.

Now here I am writing a chapter on joy and
how laughter can contribute to better health!
By this time you should realize that even I am
human! Yet, comparatively speaking, I have
much, very much to be joyful for. It has been

my opportunity to travel around the world
. . . to see the dead and dying in Vietnam, to
experience the conflicts in the Middle East, to
see Arab refugees living in tents on a forgotten desert drinking from cups swarming with
flies. I have seen the abject poverty of Cal-
cutta.

When I see misfortunes of those around me
. . . truly I have much to be joyful and thankful for. And I am!

Joy Brings Healing

The Bibles says that a joyful heart is good
medicine. What this really means is that a
joyful heart literally *causes good healing!*

This may be hard for some to understand . . .
that literally, one who is happy, one who is
joyful, one who approaches life with a positive drive . . . is actually fueling his body with
that which is conducive to good health.

We live today in an age of specialists. And we
have successfully taken the body apart and
broken it down in segments. What we fail to
realize is that God did not create our body like
General Motors puts together a car. And for
this we can be doubly thankful!

The Age of Specialists

Have you ever been to a hospital lately? There
are *right* nostril specialists and *left* nostril
specialists. And heaven help you if you get in
the wrong room!

Hospitals are now becoming human parts factories. We have done an acceptable job in
medicine but have failed miserably in treating the *whole* body. And the whole body includes soul and spirit.

I realize it will be extremely difficult for some

The Bible tells us: "For anger and rage kill the foolish man; jealousy and indignation slay the simple" (Job 5:2). How many times have you found that people whose constant attitude is one of envy and bitterness are often plagued with chronic illness.

doctors to understand this. As it will be to understand how laughter and a joyful heart can be effective in combating serious and yes, even terminal, illness.

Drop the 6-o'clock News

It was only recently that a Workshop Library on World Humor was started because a retired U.S. Foreign Service officer realized the value of laughter in a world so dominated by the depressing "6-o'clock news."

Did you ever see anyone frown when they are laughing? Impossible. I am sure you know some people who walk around all their life as though they are sucking on a lemon. Their lips are turned down, they have a perpetual frown, their forehead is furrowed with wrinkles. Nothing makes them joyful. It can be sunshiny, the birds can be singing, and the postman could have just left them a $10,000 check from their lost Uncle Ebenezer. And what would they say, if you asked them what a beautiful day today is . . .

> The weather man says it's going to rain tomorrow! Hear the racket those birds are making . . . that's a sure sign of a bitter winter ahead.

And you respond,

> But aren't you thrilled about the $10,000 Uncle Ebenezer left you?

To which they reply:

> He could have left me $50,000 . . . the old skinflint. Besides, the $10,000 will all be eaten up in taxes!

So you politely say goodbye, as you walk on your way to the hospital to visit your sick daughter who has just been diagnosed as hav-ing breast cancer. And just this morning your husband phoned to tell you he just lost his job and you may have to give up the bungalow that was your dream house and move into an apartment. And the morning mail just brought you a nice letter from I.R.S. saying they re-examined your tax return and "*Congratulations, you owe $250 more plus $35 in penalties!*"

And it is then you can understand Jeremiah's lament in Jeremiah 12:1 when he asks the Lord:

> *Why has the way of the wicked prospered?*

Count It All Joy

For a moment you feel sorry for yourself and then remember the verse in the New Testament book of James:

> *My brethren, count it all joy,*
> *when you encounter various trials,*
> *knowing that the testing of your faith produces endurance.*
> *And let endurance have its perfect result, that you may be perfect and complete,*
> *lacking in nothing.*
>
> (James 1:2-4 ASV)

COUNT IT ALL JOY! Laugh! Rejoice in spite of your illness, in spite of your circumstances! For in rejoicing, you are not allowing the poisons of depression, of bitterness, of anger, of moodiness to pollute your body. Laughter is the EXPELLANT of poisons. And the more you laugh and rejoice, the more you will be able to endure the problems along life's way.

The Secret of Living

And endurance, the Bible tells us, has its perfect result in spiritual maturity. Endurance implies "steadfastness," an ability to be on an even plane regardless of circumstances that engulf you. This remarkable ability comes about by JOY. My wife has been blessed with a remarkable gift of joy and it reflects and is rubbed off on everyone who meets her!

Recently I held a health seminar in Las Vegas, Nevada. Sorry to say, I found this city the most depressing city I have ever been in. I could not wait to leave. At the same time I attended the National Nutrition Foods Association convention held in Las Vegas. It was inconceivable to me that this organization would choose Las Vegas to have a nutrition foods convention. For what they (the nutrition foods manufacturers) are promoting is diametrically opposed to all that Las Vegas stands for!

The Profit Persuaders

It was impossible to enter the Hilton Hotel, where the convention was held, without walking through a mammoth room filled with slot machines and a gambling casino. You even had to pass through this getting to the registration desk.

There was nothing in this whole atmosphere that generated joy. By joy, I mean, *real* joy! Of course, there was plenty of artificial joy and the glaring neon signs attempted to wipe out the blackness of night. In fact, restaurants were open all night with all kinds of "joy-killing" foods!

There Was No Joy

I studied the faces of those who were gambling. There were even slot machines in the airport. And those who played them stood transfixed, literally hypnotized by these one-arm bandits. Some were old, some were on crutches . . . even some on wheelchairs. In fact, at the Hilton, they "graciously" supply motorized carts for those in ill health to commute from one gambling table to another.

I could find no joy on their faces!

As a child I remember singing a chorous:

> Jesus and
> Others and
> You

What a wonderful way to spell JOY!

And I have found this principle to be valid. It works.

It is not my desire to "impose" my spiritual beliefs on you, but simply to tell you that real joy does come through a personal acceptance of Jesus Christ as Saviour and Lord.

Laughter . . . Good and Bad

Now what about laughter? Laughter is a normal byproduct of joy.

Not all laughter is beneficial. It's much like the mushroom and the toadstool.

There is laughter in Las Vegas, when someone wins a few dollars. There is laughter at the race track, when someone's horse wins. There is raucous laughter in the locker room when someone tells an off-color joke. There is the leering laughter when someone laughs because of someone's physical or mental incapacities. This is toadstool laughter. It is poisonous to your body and to your soul and to your spirit!

There is laughter in a wedding, when two couples unite. There is laughter at the birth of a child. There is laughter at the cute antics of a child. There is laughter at a family reunion. There is laughter at a graduation. There is laughter when friends get together. There is laughter at a humorous story that is uplifting or wholesome. This is mushroom laughter. It is food for your body, for your soul, for your spirit!

A Fine Line

Laughter and tears are just a hairsbreadth apart. And sometimes they are almost simultaneous! A recent vivid example comes to my mind.

Our daughter, Diane, felt led to go to Prairie Bible Institute in Three Hills, Alberta, Canada. We live in a suburb of Philadelphia . . . way across the other side of the continent. Three Hills is about 500 miles north of Spokane, Washington.

She had never been away from home before. My wife and I saw her off at the airport right after Christmas, 1976. We well remember that day. As she said goodbye, just prior to boarding the plane, we all cried!

Then, in July, 1977, my wife and I decided to surprise Diane by flying in to see her. We arrived in Three Hills about 3 PM on a Saturday afternoon. She did not know we were coming.

The Surprise

We walked down the hall of the school building to where her room was. There was a light in her room. The door was slightly ajar. We could see her their studying by the light of a

I took this photo at the moment our daughter, Diane, embraced her mother. Reunion occurred in dining room of Prairie Bible Institute, April, 1977. To the left of Diane is our daughter, Doreen, holding her son, Joshua. Doreen's other child, Jessica, is in my wife's arms.

It was a joyous reunion. Our whole family was there. Back to camera is son, Duane. Note the expression of joy on the face of my wife, Mary and the tears of joy on the face of Diane.

desk lamp. Slowly I pushed the door opened.

Suddenly she looked up and saw my wife and me standing there at her door. I wish you could have seen the expression on her face. It was one of shock and surprise. Her jaw dropped. Her eyes widened. There was a moment of complete silence. Suddenly she rose from her chair, hugged her mother. And both began crying and laughing at the same time!

A Cherished Experience

It was an experience all of us will always cherish.

I can remember another time. Our daughter, Doreen and her husband, Wes, moved out to the state of Washington. The first time my wife and I visited them, they did not know we were coming. They lived on the side of a mountain in a log-type cabin with no modern facilities. We drove up a 2-mile dirt road to their home but they were not there.

A Joyful Reunion

We waited behind a trailer at their home until their truck drove up. As Doreen got out of the truck with her children, I told my wife to come from behind the trailer and I would snap a photo of this joyful reunion. Again there were tears and laughter intermingled.

Perhaps you have heard the expression TEARS OF JOY. And tears can be joyful. And laughter can be the world's best medicine for you! Laughter can heal you!

Now I am sure that some doctors will dispute the fact that laughter can heal you. But I believe it. Some will point out that laughter can kill you. They will say that too much laughing may cause *cataplexy*, which is an attack of sudden weakness and collapse. But this is an extremely rare and exotic condition.

Now laughter may kill you if you drive the wrong way down a turnpike and laugh as you go head-on into a Greyhound bus!

But healthy laughter is an essential ingredient in a back-to-nature diet. Most people just think of food in a nutritional program. However, be sure to include a JOYFUL HEART . . . one that is grateful for the blessings . . . and a MERRY HEART . . . one that can laugh in spite of what may appear to be adverse circumstances!

Laughing Back to Health

Norman Cousins did that! He laughed his way back to good health! Norman Cousins is editor of the Saturday Review. One day specialists informed him he was suffering from a painful disease called

Ankylosing Spondylitis
(Marie-Strumpell Disease)

Ankylosing Spondylititis is a chronic, progressive disease of the small joints of the spine. The spine becomes immobile. Often there is diminished chest expansion. Demineralization occurs and finally, the characteristic "bamboo spine." In the past this has been treated by corticosteroids, gold therapy and irradiation therapy. It was found that irradiation therapy greatly increased the risk of leukemia.

Doctors now treat it with two other drugs: phenylbutazone and indomethacin.

**The
Side
Effects**

Phenylbutazone side effects include:

Bone marrow depression
Kidney damage, Hepatitis
Ulcers
Eye damage, possible impaired
vision
Ear damage, possible hearing loss
Mental and behavioral disturbance

It should be noted that this drug does not correct the underlying disease process!

Indomethacin has many similar side effects and the drug companies are not sure where this drug action takes place or the method of its action on the human body.

Now Norman Cousins found himself lying flat on his back with all the bones in his spine and joints hurting.

**Poor Chance
of
Recovery**

Specialists told him that his chances of recovery were 1 in 500 and they said they personally never witnessed a cure!

Norman Counsins had plenty of time on his hands, bedfast. So he began to wonder. He reasoned:

*It was easy enough to hope and love
and have faith, but what about
laughter? Nothing is less funny than
being flat on your back with all the
bones in your spine and joints hurting.*

Cousins decided to try an experiment. He was able to obtain some films of Allen Funt's old CANDID CAMERA television show. A nurse ran the projector for him.

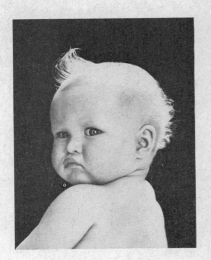

Why go through your entire life looking as though you had just swallowed a lemon?

If life hands you a lemon ... make lemonade. It just may be possible for you to laugh your way back to better health!

**A
Laughing
Discovery**

And Cousins proceeded to LAUGH!

He was amazed at the results. He exclaimed:

> It worked!

> I made the joyous discovery that 10 minutes of genuine belly laughter would give me hours of pain-free sleep. When the pain-killing effect of the laughter wore off, we would switch on the motion picture projector again and, not infrequently, it would lead to another pain-free sleep interval.

However, his belly laughs began to annoy the other patients in the hospital. So he removed himself to a hotel room, where the "treatment" was continued.

Along with laughter he took large doses of Vitamin C. And he got better!

**Again the
Doubters**

This unusual story was written up in the staid New England Journal of Medicine. And as expected, an "authority on pain" from the department of neurosurgery at Chicago's Rush Medical College, upon hearing of this unusual treatment, remarked:

> Obviously he didn't have an incurable disease, which makes the diagnosis suspect. ... We know that under stress the body acts in certain definite ways. I don't know of anything specifically that says if you laugh you reverse the effects.

Obviously this neurosurgeon has not read and understood Proverbs 17:22 (ASV);

> A joyful heart is good medicine

**The Bible
Has
The Answer**

This literally means that a joyful heart causes good healing! The Bible can be no more positive. In that same verse we are told:

But a broken spirit dries up the bones

What a beautiful application this makes to Norman Cousins whose spine bones were fusing because the liquid was drying up! How many people may be suffering from arthritis because their spirit is broken . . . their life is lacking in joy and laughter!

I admit if someone is inserting in your body Phyenylbutazone and Indomethacin it can quickly rob you of your joy! Does Ankylosing Spondylitis occur because your body is lacking in Phyenylbutazone and Indomethacin? (or any other disease, for that matter?) I prefer to believe not!

I realize that some doctors will have a most difficult time believing that laughter and Vitamin C can reverse an illness. But I am reminded of what the Bible tells us in the New Testament in I Corinthians 1:27:

*God has chosen the foolish things of
the world to shame the wise . . .*

It was Joseph Addison who said:

*Man is distinguished from all other
creatures by the faculty of laughter.*

Now I am not suggesting you laugh all day when your doctor tells you that you have an inoperable cancer. What I am suggesting is that you face each new day with a joyful, positive, happy attitude. Let your face beam with happiness and laughter . . . for your face will be a mirror of your insides.

When Men Cry

When the Democrats won the election, Abraham Lincoln was asked how he felt about the results. He was quoted as saying:

> *Somewhat like the boy in Kentucky, who stubbed his toe while running to see his sweetheart. The boy said he was too big to cry, and far too badly hurt to laugh.*

Which leads me to another point. Crying is also conducive to good health. Men should also cry. For in crying we release our inner tensions and emotions. There is, as I said before, a thin line between tears and joy.

I would not expect you to break out with a belly laugh the moment the doctor advises you that you have cancer. (He may also suggest a psychiatrist) But calmly, thank him for his observation and rejoice in the news! The Bible tells us:

> *In everything give thanks . . .*
>   (1 Thessalonians 5:18)

The Everything of Everything

Everything means **everything**. Our family practices this. And we know it works!

The most utterly lost of all days is the one in which you have not once laughed. It has been my opportunity to speak in many churches throughout the United States. I try to inject some purposeful humor in my messages. And infrequently someone will get up from the audience and angrily stomp out the door. I feel sorry for those who cannot laugh and whose lives do not radiate joy!

Three Degrees of Laughter

It has been said that there are three degrees of laughter:

> The lowest is the laughter of a man who laughs at his own jokes.
>
> Next is the laughter of a man who laughs at the jokes of others.
>
> But the highest and finest of all is the laughter of a man who laughs at himself.

Dr. James J. Walsh of Fordham University said:

> People who laugh actually live longer than those who don't laugh.
>
> Few persons realize that health actually varies according to the amount of laughter.

A Good Prescription

Would a doctor be arrested for malpractice if he suggested to a cancer patient:

> Take two Marx Brothers and Three Stooges, and if that doesn't help have one Lucille Ball and an orange!

Well, it is now 3 PM. It is still gloomy outdoors. The air conditioner still doesn't work. And I am hot. But honestly, as I got into this subject I really became inspired and started chuckling myself.

By the way, did you hear the joke about the doctor who came home and found his cellar flooded.

Quickly he called his plumber and explained his dilemma. The plumber said that he was busy and could not come over for a couple days.

I need help right now!
Why the water is already up to my
waist in the basement and soon will
flood the kitchen! What shall I do?

To which the plumber calmly replied:

Take two aspirin and get plenty of
bed rest!

MEETING SOME NEW FRIENDS . . .

I am surprised how many people don't know what Lentils are! And when you mention Okra . . . they look at you with a blank expression that sometimes turns into one of sympathy or pity (or both).

Very few people eat Eggplant and fewer still know how they grow. No, they are not eggs planted by chickens!

And if Eggplant seems slighted, what about Millet and Comfrey? No wonder you have never seen an Eggplant smile!

English scholars will wonder why I capitalize each of these vegetables. I do so because I think it is high time they receive the attention they deserve!

The next few chapters will acquaint you with highly nutritious foods that are also very tasty when prepared properly. These foods are the basics of a GETTING BACK TO NATURE DIET. **Incorporate them in your diet and you will have taken the first step towards a healthy body.**

The last few chapters reveal how to walk the path to better health by discovering life's true values. **Incorporate these suggestions in your own life and you will have taken the first step towards a healthy mind.**

It is my hope that these chapters might change your life . . . for the better. And if this occurs, don't keep the secret to yourself. Give **THE GETTING BACK TO NATURE DIET** book to your loved ones and friends . . . particularly those who are ill. Daily our newspapers and television confront us with bad news. Why not reverse the trend? And pass on some good news to help lift up a friend. A person is never so tall as when he stoops to help others.

Salem Kirban

4

HAVE YOU EVER SEEN AN EGGPLANT SMILE?

**Doesn't
Anyone
Love an
Eggplant?**

Believe me when I tell you, there is no egg in Eggplant!

Have you ever seen an Eggplant plant? It is a most unusual plant. They generally grow about two to four feet tall and each plant yields an average of 3 Eggplants. You wonder how such a small plant can support such a large Eggplant.

Eggplants have a tough life. But they bounce back with resiliency. Every day millions of Americans buy hamburgers and french fries. But suggest Eggplant and they turn their noses at the mere mention of the name.

Eggplant is almost (but not quite) equal to Okra in the list of citizens without a country.

I feel sorry for the Eggplant. It is saddled with such an odd name. It has such an odd shape. It is never given "equal rights" in the supermarket produce section (and the Okra is even more neglected). Eggplant has become a second class citizen. I believe vegetables should organize a lobby group called CORE; Committee On Rights for the Eggplant.

purple thick eggplant

The Middle East priest was so impressed by the Eggplant dish his
fiancée prepared for him that he requested that her dowry be the
oil in which to cook it.

**The
Poor Man's
Meat**

I've never seen Eggplant be pushy like a watermelon. Those watermelon carry a lot of weight! And I believe the least we can do is to capitalize Eggplant wherever it appears. Like Okra, it's an honor long past due!

Eggplant (*Solanum melongena*) is known by the English as Aubergine. We Lebanese call it, *betingan* (but-n-gen). I can still smell that fragrant aroma of Eggplant cooking in garlic and olive oil. My mother never had to call me in for supper.

Eggplant is often called the "poor man's meat." Maybe that's why our family had it so much during the Depression. We were too naive to believe it was a poor man's food. To us it was a delicacy which we could enjoy in abundance from our garden at minimal cost.

The Eggplant is a distant relative to the potato. It is said to have originated in India. Unlike most garden vegetables, no wild plant has ever been found of the Eggplant.

The Eggplant was unknown to the Greeks and the Romans.

**The Eggplant
and Love**

There is an interesting story about Eggplant. An imam or priest in the Middle East was so impressed by the Eggplant dish his fiancée prepared for him that he requested that her dowry be the oil in which to cook it! In those days it was a custom for the bride's parents to pay the husband for marrying their daughter. And the dowry was the property that a woman brings to her husband at marriage.

The new husband had large Ali Baba-type jars of oil stored in their new home. As is the usual custom, the Eggplant slices were immersed in this oil.

The first and second nights the wife prepared the Eggplant it was delicious. But on the third night the husband found no Eggplant dish awaiting him.

Tragedy in the Kitchen

"Alas," said his wife, *"the first two nights have exhausted the supply of oil."* The husband fainted!

What many people do not realize is that Eggplant slices are highly absorbant. The tale goes on that the priest Imam Bayeldi had a thousand wives. And whenever they served a dinner of Eggplant he swooned with ecstasy!

Today that dish is called *Imam Bayeldi* and the recipe appears at the end of this chapter.

Fashionable Oriental ladies once made a black dye with eggplant. The dye was used to stain ladies' teeth which were polished until they gleamed like metal.

Eggplants appeared in Europe in the 14th century, probably by way of Africa. It is mentioned by an Arab physician in the 13th century. From Europe, the cultivation of Eggplant spread to America. There are old documents to show that it was cultivated in Brazil as early as 1658.

Many Italian dishes use the Eggplant. This unusual vegetable was introduced in Italy towards the end of the 14th century.

The Eggplant is not well known in the North because its cultivation requires warmth and constant and abundant irrigation. However, we live in a suburb of Philadelphia and I have no trouble growing a great harvest of Eggplant every year without any watering except nature's rainfall. The Eggplant is a very hardy plant and quite disease free.

The Secret of the Sepal

eggplant flower

The flowers of an Eggplant are very beautiful. They are star-shaped, a typical blue-violet color, with five petals and five sepals. You don't know what a sepal is? I challenge you to look it up in the dictionary ... right now. This would be a marvelous time to get acquainted with the Eggplant and its sepals. Every Eggplant you buy is hugged by 5 sepals! Think of that momentous discovery! I would venture to say that even the President of the United States does not know that fact! And here the Arabs and Israeli's are feuding with each other. They both eat Eggplant. Maybe they should look at what they are eating (before it is cut up). The Eggplant with its sepals has a real message for us ... a simple message of companionship and love.

Housewives through the centuries have always placed sliced Eggplant on a cloth to dry after sprinkling the slices with salt. The purpose: to draw off the excess water.

Some thought that the unripe Eggplant contained potentially dangerous amounts of solanine (which is a poisonous narcotic obtained from potato sprouts and tomatoes). This insinuation was unfortunate for the poor Eggplant and just one of the nasty rumors that have been used through the centuries to make it disreputable.

How the Eggplant Became the Apple of Love

Dr. Carlton Fredericks, in his book, <u>Look Younger, Feel Healthier</u>, (p. 235) states:

> *The best illustration (of superstition) is the twentieth-century housewife, who is preparing Eggplant salts the slices and then stacks them to let the liquid drain. Her custom dates directly from the twelfth century and has changed little since. It was believed that the juice of the Eggplant had the capacity to cause insanity — particularly in doctors and lawyers. So, it is, that this practice of the twelfth-century housewife, in protecting her family against the juice of insanity, is still employed today. All that we have done is to discard the original name for the eggplant, which directly reflected the superstition, the apple of insanity.*

Yet, oddly enough, the Spaniards of the 16th century called eggplants "apples of love."

Perhaps that is why, in cooking, we have desecrated the Eggplant by camouflaging it with bread crumbs, cheese, and tomatoes and by crushing and burying it in a casserole. And the greatest insult to injury is the frying of Eggplant!

My Favorite Recipe

Here is my favorite preparation of Eggplant. I take a whole Eggplant and slice it horizontally in 3/4" slices. I dip this in olive oil that is saturated with freshly crushed garlic. Since Eggplant is very absorbant it drinks in this flavorful liquid quickly. Then I sprinkle garlic or onion powder on these wet slices along with cayenne pepper.

This is placed on a barbecue grill and grilled about 5-7 minutes on each side of a hot fire. It comes out crisp and crunchy with that indescribable barbecue flavor. If you can't barbecue it, try broiling or baking it the same way.

My mother used to stuff Eggplant. They can be stuffed a variety of ways. The pulp is scooped out and a filling of onions, ground lamb, cinnamon and pine nuts are generally inserted. This is slowly simmered or baked.

Eggplant Good for Health

Therapeutically, the Eggplant has been used for anemia, constipation, to promote flow of urine, to aid the function of the liver and pancreas and to calm one who exhibits anxiety.

Perhaps the greatest anxiety is caused by those who are still looking for the egg in Eggplant. And when some frustrated housewives can't find it, they crack an egg over the poor Eggplant slice and ruin it!

If you haven't done your good deed today, here's your chance. The next time you are in the supermarket, take a Magic Marker pen and make the sign over the Eggplant a capital "E". And then push the vegetables around it aside to give Eggplant a wider and more prominent berth.

Have you ever seen an Eggplant smile? This week, tell an Eggplant a joke! Help brighten its life. Let's be unusually kind to Eggplants from now on. Who knows? The Eggplant you save, may be your own!

EGGPLANT PARTY DIP
(Baba Ghanoush)
10 Servings

First prepare eggplant purée by cooking on barbecue grill (or broiler):

3 eggplants

until skins start to blister and flesh is soft and juicy. Rub skins off under cold water. Gently squeeze eggplant to eliminate some of its natural juices (which are sometimes bitter).

Mash eggplants as you would mash potatoes. Then add:

4 crushed garlic cloves
½ teaspoon garlic salt

Pound this mixture (crushed garlic and eggplant) into a smooth, creamy purée. You may wish to use a blender for this. While blending, add:

½ cup tahini*
Juice of 3 lemons

Taste, and if necessary add more tahini or lemon and garlic to give delicate yet sharp flavor. Pour mixture into bowl or small serving dishes and garnish with chopped parsley, black olives and chopped pimento. Serve with flat Arab bread or unsalted crackers.

Tahini is a crushed sesame butter with a yogurt-like consistency. It can be purchased in your health food store and some supermarkets.

EGGPLANT a la IMAM BAYILDI
6 Servings

First prepare filling by sautéing:

¾ lb. onions sliced thinly

in:

4 tablespoons olive oil

Add:

3 large cloves garlic crushed

Remove from heat and stir in:

½ cup parsley chopped
1 teaspoon mint
¾ cup tomatoes chopped

Season to taste, mix well.

Prepare:

6 long medium-sized eggplants

by cutting slice off stem end and saving this to act as "cork." Scoop out the pulp with knife or pointed grapefruit-type spoon. Be careful not to break through skin. (Pulp can be saved for salad or stew) Sprinkle inside of eggplant shell with garlic salt. Leave inverted in a colander for 1/2 hour to drain.

Stuff eggplant with:

filling previously prepared.

Close them with reserved "cork." Arrange eggplant side by side in large pan.

Pour over them:

½ cup olive oil

mixed with juice of:

1 lemon

Salt lightly with:

Garlic salt

Cover pan and simmer gently for about 1 hour until eggplants are very soft. Remove from heat. May be served warm or allow to cool and serve as a cold dish.

EGGPLANT/SPINACH SALAD
6 Servings

Discover:
1 medium-sized eggplant
Slice lengthwise in 1/2" slices.
Rub lemon juice over both sides
of slices. Then cut into 1/2"
cubes. Steam for 5 minutes. Place
cubes in chilled container. Re-
frigerate for 1 hour.
In large salad bowl add:
10 spinach leaves chopped
1 cup bean or alfalfa sprouts
¼ cup raw sunflower seeds
1 tomato chopped
½ teaspoon garlic salt
Mix above thoroughly, then add:
chilled eggplant cubes
Add your favorite dressing but
include **juice of 1 fresh lemon.**
For sparkle, I dare you to dust
with **cayenne pepper!**

Salem's
GRILLED EGGPLANT SLICES
4 Servings

Select:
1 medium-sized egglpant
Lay eggplant on side and cut into 3/4"
slices, leaving skin on! Brush both
sides of eggplant abundantly with
Salem's Golden Glow* (so that it
soaks in). Sprinkle these saturated
sparkling slices with **garlic salt** and a
light **dash of cayenne pepper.** Place
on barbecue grill and cook each side
till browned (about 7 minutes on hot
fire). **OR,** if you have no barbecue,
broil in oven till done.

* Golden Glow is made by taking **4-5
cloves of garlic,** slicing them thin on
a saucer that has about 5 tablespoons
of olive oil. **Crush** the **garlic** in **oil**
and mix together so aroma of garlic
blends with oil. Then **pour** this essence into a **cup of olive oil.** Mix
thoroughly! And there you have
Salem's Golden Glow ready to brush
your eggplant. (The same Golden
Glow technique can be used as a
dressing for salads!)

Select:
1 medium-sized eggplant
Lay eggplant on side and cut into 3/4"
slices, leaving skin on! Brush both
sides of eggplant abundantly with
Salem's Golden Glow* (so that it
soaks in. Sprinkle these saturated
sparkling slices with **garlic salt** and a
light **dash of cayenne pepper.** Place
on barbeque grill and cook each side
till browned (about 7 minutes on hot
fire). **OR,** if you have no barbeque,
broil in oven till done.

* Golden Glow is made by taking **4-5
cloves of garlic,** slicing them thin on
a saucer that has about 5 tablespoons
of olive oil. **Crush** the **garlic** in **oil**
and mix together so aroma of garlic
blends with oil perfect marriage.
Then **pour** this essence into a **cup of
olive oil.** Mix thoroughly! and There
you have **Salem's Golden Glow**
ready to brush your eggplant. (The
same Golden Glow technique can be
used as a dressing for salads!)

AUNT EFFIE . . .
Did you hear about the egg in the monastery?

Yes! Out of the frying pan and into the frier! But people seem to know more about eggs than eggplant. No wonder you never see an eggplant smile! People are creatures of habit. Habit is a cable; we weave a thread for it each day and it becomes so strong that we cannot break it! Habit is the whip that makes the man of today obey the boy of yesterday! And too many parents have developed their children's tastebuds for them.

"Eat an eggplant? My NO . . . Johnny doesn't like that!" No wonder the way you cook this precious vegetable. You fry it masking its delicate flavor with breading or gooky eggs or buy those pathetic misfits some supermarkets call eggplant.

The Spaniards, bless their hearts, knew the eggplant was the apple of love. Why it contains 10 precious minerals all ready to be released just as soon as you take one succulent bite. And it's loaded with Vitamin C. Eating eggplant can help your digestion, too!

If you really want to live, try slicing eggplant nice and thick and placing it on a barbecue grill. Every once in a while Salem Kirban invites me over when he's barbecuing eggplant. But he's stingy. He only gives me 1 slice and keeps 3 for himself.

5

HOW TO END A WAR WITH CELERY

**The Key
to Peace**

I think I have found the key to peace! Supply every world leader with a stalk of celery every day!

Celery is the world's greatest and most natural tranquilizer.

Americans ingest more than 50 million tablets of aspirin a day! And aspirin (*acetylsalicylic acid*) is the primary ingredient in over 50,000 over-the-counter (nonprescription) drugs now available in the U.S. Over 300 million prescriptions a year are filled for tranquilizers in the United States! Librium, Valium, Miltown, Equanil, etc. are all anti-anxiety drugs.

**The
Profit
Pushers**

Those who don't submerge their troubles in tranquilizers drown themselves in alcohol; a $2 billion business in America! Liquor companies, dismayed by what they term "insufficient sales" are boosting their advertising budget. In 1977 Seagrams was allocating $40 million in magazines alone to push 7 Crown, Seagram VO and Crown Royal. This is called "the most aggressive marketing program in the history of the distilled spirits industry."

There are increasing problems in the world today that make it much more difficult for a person to cope with life than in the 18th or 19th century. Wide open spaces are disappearing and population explosion creates crowded conditions in most cities and suburbs. Air pollution tends to encourage chronic diseases such as asthma, allergies and emphysema.

We Are Slaves To Time

What were simple, quick processes before now become a monumental hurdle. A TV commercial shows a leading personality jumping over the counter and picking up his Hertz rental key in a split second. But anyone who has rented cars knows this is more fiction than fact. Generally, there is a substantial wait and getting to the car in the large airports can involve anywhere from 1/2 to 1 hour in time!

Then there's the problem of trying to get appliances serviced. Many large chain stores claim top service for their appliances. However, I have found the opposite in most cases. Most of this book was written when our central air conditioner was broken. I sat perspiring in my small library trying to be creative. Now I know why writing is 5% inspiration and 95% perspiration. When I first called for service (and getting them on the phone is a project in itself) . . . we were told the serviceman would come in 10 days. I knew the motor was shot. So in desperation I called their Chicago office. They got the appointment moved up to 6 days. The serviceman came, looked at the motor and said,

"It's broken ... and even if we had a new motor it would take 12 more days to put it in."

When Patience Wears Thin

Six days for me to wait for him to tell me the motor was broken! That's why I called them in the first place! Again I placed a long distance call, this time to the Secretary to the President. In about 6 more days they came with a motor. It worked 1 hour! That was last Thursday. Today, Monday, I called Chicago again. And I am still waiting.

Now I can live without an air conditioner. I lived without one for some 30 years. And I have experienced the hot humid days and nights of Vietnam. But I guess the thing that irritated me was that hardly a month goes by that some telephone solicitor is not calling us to sell us a service contract on our dryer or washer or refrigerator or a special combination contract. So when I called service, I wanted it in a reasonable time ... not when the first snowfall comes. For what I have paid in service contracts I could have purchased a new central air conditioning unit!

Now I am telling you all this just to give you an example of how daily irritations like this make it more difficult to cope in today's world. I am sure you have had the same type of experiences.

Last night, as an example, was a night our whole family looked forward to. Our daughter, Dawn, had spent 7 weeks as a teen missionary helping construct a building for missionaries in Venezuela. Finally, she was coming home. She was supposed to come home on Tuesday, August 9th. But when her group arrived in Caracas airport they were told there would be a delay. They had overbooked. Finally, they put her on a plane on Sunday, August 14th. That day someone decided to try to bomb a Venezuelan plane in Miami and her plane was delayed in landing because one runway was inoperative.

The Frustrations of Life

As we drove down in our new car, the engine sputtered and died. I had taken the car back to the dealer on 4 different occasions and asked them why my engine light on the dashboard kept blinking on. They assured me nothing was wrong. Now, as we were about to have a reunion at the airport after a 7 week separation . . . the car absolutely leaves us. Frustration! It was running as though someone had put tin cans in the motor. We had to return home and get another car.

Just minor, everyday occurrences. But nonetheless irritations that annoy. I've learned to be resilient and to follow the Scripture admonition:

> in everything give thanks . . .
> (1 Thessalonians 5:18 KJV)

but I am still human and sometimes the lack of efficiency on the part of others and their lack of concern gets the best of me.

When travelling overseas and a minor difficulty arises, such as trying to change a plane schedule or take photographs inside the Garden of Gethsemane, the first word that comes out of the mouth of the other individual is usually:

IMPOSSIBLE!

The emphasis is usually on the first syllable and they say

EEEEMMPOSSEEEBUL!

Then, cooly, calmly and collectively I say to them:

> Now that we have determined that
> this is impossible . . . let us now seek
> to find a way to make it POSSIBLE!

Or have you ever had someone say:

> We can't do it. It's company policy!

Our World is Run by Policy

I usually reply:

> Policy is not an inanimate object.
> Policy is made by people.
> And the people who make a policy
>   can also <u>change</u> that policy!

This may be a long way around to say that we do live in a more difficult world. And unless one knows how to cope with it . . . one can fall apart and resort to drugs (legal or illegal), cigarettes and alcohol or withdraw from society.

The Secret Word

If I could select one word as the secret of coping with living in the modern 20th Century world . . . I would select the word:

RESILIENCY

Resiliency is that ability to bounce or spring back . . . an ability to recover your strength and your spirits quickly. Resiliency gives you

Government sources indicate that fast-food outlets are now over 47,000 strong. McDonalds is the largest chain, with 4600 units nationwide . . . Kentucky Fried Chicken has lined the landscape with more than 4000 of its red-and-white-striped buildings . . . Pizza Hut dishes out millions of Italian pies each day in the more than 2,500 restaurants it has established.

In 1970 McDonald's invested $18.5 million to advertise its burger bill of fare: by 1976 the ad budget — most of it devoted to TV — had expanded 450 percent to $100 million! McDonald's sales in 1976 were $2,470,000,000.

Kentucky Fried Chicken, not about to be left behind . . . also raised its TV and billboard ante 450 percent, to $55 million.

The Agricultural Department informs us that we eat one of three meals away from home (By 1980, we will feed ourselves one meal in a restaurant for every meal we eat at home.)

Our adoration of candy is reflected by the awesome size of the confectionary business in America. According to the U.S. Department of Commerce we ate more than 3.4 billion pounds of candy in 1975. For this pleasure, we shelled out close to 3 billion dollars. That's a nationwide average of 16.3 pounds per person.[1]

[1] Michael S. Lasky, The Complete Junk Food Book
   (New York: McGraw-Hill Book Company), 1977, pp. 101, 102, 48.

a buoyancy to meet the problems of life[1] head-on and live <u>above</u> one's circumstances. While some may question whether there are any side effects from taking marijuana or other drugs including Valium, etc. — that is <u>not</u> the point. The point is that the ingesting of these drugs indicates we are cowards, unable to face squarely our problems and turn each problem into a SOLUTION.

The Rebound of Deadly Diets

One of the basic reasons one cannot cope with today's problems is because of today's diet. We are feeding our body junk foods and television is feeding our mind with an equal amount of garbage. Is it no wonder that half of America is on tranquilizers of one type or another. Right now we are almost hypnotized for a world leader to come in and take us over to run us like automatons!

Because our present-day diets, for the most part, leave us physical misfits, we run to the doctor for that miracle pill that will make the world rosy again. We certainly would feel cheated if he told us to go to the supermarket and buy a couple stalks of celery and chew on them.

Yet, in my opinion, <u>THAT IS THE ANSWER!</u>

"Oh," you say, *"come now, that's much too simple!"*

Of course, it's simple!

Your body does not suffer from a lack of Valium! It does suffer from a lack of nutrients.

---

[1] Anyone who has read some of my over 30 books knows that I place faith in God as the first requisite for living in today's world. My testimony to this can be found in Goodbye Mr. President, $2.95.

**The Benefits
of
Celery**

And celery is rich in magnesium, sodium and iron. It is an excellent tonic to sooth one's jangled nerves! It is also conducive to sound sleep.

Celery can be traced back to the Greeks and Romans. In fact they thought so highly of celery that they used it to crown the heads of distinguished guests.

In 800 B.C. celery was mentioned in Homers Odyssey as *selinon*. During the first century, Dioscorides, a renowned Greek author, praised celery for its sedative properties. The ancient Greeks awarded celery for sporting achievements. (This might be cheaper than paying a million dollars to a star football player!)

**A
Blood
Purifier**

As late as the 16th century, celery was identified as a medicinal plant only. And as late as 1722, celery was still referred to as

a herb eaten to purify the blood.

The Chinese also used celery as a medicine.

Cultivation of celery as a food crop apparently began in the 16th century in Italy and northern Europe. Its use in the kitchen at that time was primarily as a flavoring. By 1726 celery seed was sold in England for planting for use in soups and broths. And by the middle of the 17th century people began to eat even the celery stalks and leaves with an oil dressing as a type of salad!

By the early 1800's celery made its way to America. Celery was such a novelty that enterprising Dutch/American gardeners at Kalamazoo, Michigan, displayed celery on the railway station for sale to passengers on the train. The news spread quickly about this appetizing food and the demand for it increased.

The people of England and other parts of Europe were more accustomed to the white or blanched celery. In America it was discovered how to grow a celery that ripens green. The green celery, of course, has a high content of nutritious Vitamin A, which is not present after a crop is blanched.

Medical herbalists today still use celery for their carminative (gas expelling) ability and the benefits they exert upon the kidneys.

Don't Throw Away the Leaves

The leaves of celery have the highest content of Vitamin C. Celery is very rich in Vitamin A and potassium.

In a study among those who wanted to lose weight, volunteers were allowed to eat anything they desired. But they had to agree to eat one average size bunch of celery per day by eating it before and between meals.

In these tests a moderate weight reduction was achieved![2] And, I might add, the generous amount of nutrients was an added blessing!

The word "celery" can be translated from the latin, *Selinum* or *Apium graveolens var.dulce,* as quick-acting.

Celery is known for its ability to stabilize stomach function, build healthy blood cells, promote normal kidney function and provide energy. Some believe it to have an anti-arthritic action and, of course, it is excellent for calming the nerves and easing tension.

I can remember when Henry Kissinger was trying to achieve peace in the Yom Kippur War between Israel and Syria. He flew back and forth between these two countries about 30 times in a period of little over one month carrying messages to Premier Assad and Golda Meier.

When World Leaders Eat Celery

How much more sensible it would have been for both Meier and Assad to get together in Jerusalem and sit at a little table atop the Mount of Olives near the Intercontinental Hotel and (as the sun rose) breakfast on a meal of bagels and lox and Turkish coffee and happily crunch on a crisp stalk of zesty celery! There is something about crunching on celery, with that satisfying crackling sound, that wipes out one's inner hostilities. And the eating of it . . . well that just makes a roaring lion as calm as a lamb!

May I be so bold as to suggest the easiest way to end the war is to have the leaders all simultaneously chew on stalks of celery. It should be standard rations for every army, too. And instead of stalking human beings with rifles and neutron bombs, we can start stalking celery with fertilizers and transplanting rigs!

But, of course, that's too simple!

CELERY/Almond/CARROT Soup
6 Servings

In 3-quart pot, cook:
- **2 quarts chicken broth**
- **2 cups celery with leaves**
  (dice celery and leaves)
- **1 cup carrots diced**
- **½ cup onion diced**

Simmer 10 minutes, then add:
- **¼ cup butter**

Add gradually:
- **¼ cup flour**

Cook until thickened, stirring constantly. Add:
- **¾ cup almonds, ground.**

Serve sprinkling with parsley. For added zest, lightly dust each serving with cayenne pepper.

CELERY SALAD SUPREME
4 Servings

With exuberance and joy, toss together:
- **2 stalks celery with leaves**
  chopped
- **6 lettuce leaves chopped**
- **2 carrots thinly chopped**
- **1 scallion (or leek) chopped**
- **1 teaspoon almond meal**
- **2 teaspoons fresh mint**
  chopped
- **4 sprigs parsley chopped**
- **¼ cup almond pieces**
- **1 small summer squash**
  chopped

Add your favorite salad dressing. Why not try **olive oil**? Also add the **juice from 1 fresh lemon.**

CELERY/RAISIN/NUT SALAD
4 Servings

With great anticipation, toss:
- **2 cups celery diced**
- **1 cup raisins chopped**
- **1 cup nuts chopped**
- **3 tablespoons orange juice**
- **2 teaspoons lemon juice**

Allow to marinate for half an hour in the refrigerator. Drain and arrange on lettuce bed.

CELERY and CABBAGE CASSEROLE
6 Servings

With delight, cook:
- **1 cup celery chopped**

in:
- **6 tablespoons butter**

for 10 minutes, stirring frequently. Then add:
- **3½ cups cabbage chopped**

and cook 10 minutes longer. Pour into greased baking dish. Then add to taste:
- **¼ teaspoon garlic powder**
- **½ teaspoon thyme**
- **½ teaspoon oregano**
- **1 tablespoon pimineto**
  chopped

Plus:
- **1 cup white sauce***

Sprinkle over top:
- **¼ cup bread crumbs dotted**
  with 2 tablespoons butter.

Bake in moderate oven (350° F) about 20 minutes.

* White sauce is made with:
2 tablespoons butter, 2 tablespoons flour, 1 cup milk, 1/2 teaspoon herb seasoning. Melt **butter** and blend in **flour.** Add **milk** gradually, stirring constantly. Reduce heat and cook 3 minutes longer. Then add **seasoning.**

AUNT EFFIE . . .
Did you hear that Cora Mae broke off her engagement with that young doctor? And he actually asked her to return all his presents! Not only that, he sent her a bill for 35 house calls!

Serves her right! She's more nervous than a hummingbird alighting on a hot match! She's so high strung that she could go to a masquerade party as a tennis racket. She has never been able to sacrifice her appetite on the altar of appearance. Cora Mae's no good at counting calories and she has the figure to prove it!

She needs to lose weight and not by appetite depressants either! I'll never understand why everybody thinks celery is only to be chopped up in some chicken salad. Celery is an ideal food for those who are watching those unwanted pounds. And Cora Mae should start snacking on celery stalks instead of Hershey bars and Twinkies!

Celery is rich in magnesium (that reduces cholesterol) and manganese. Manganese controls the nerves in one's body and hers need controlling! And it has phosphorus, too. That's good as a nerve builder. She should run some celery through a juicer and drink about 4 ounces twice a day. It's an excellent diuretic, and will start flushing out the poisons as it calms her nerves. Good for her arthritis, too!

6

YOGURT . . . Peace Maker for the Body

**The
Yogurt
of My
Youth**

It was one of those lazy summer days in the exciting, bustling town of Schultzville, Pennsylvania (population about 50 people).

I was a mere lad of 10. Our family lived in one-half of an old house that must have been built during the Civil war. The house was on an 80-acre farm owned by a kind lady we called "Teenie."

Down by the barn was a small pond. And I can remember trying my skill at fishing. It wasn't long before I caught several small fish we called "butter fish."

Proudly I brought them home and placed them in a pan atop the ice box on the back lawn. When I went to show my mother my catch, all that was left were skeletons. It seems our cat "Yowler" had appropriated the harvest!

I can still see that familiar cheesecloth-like bag hanging from the back door near the ice box. It was my introduction to Laban (lah-bin), the Lebanese name for what you would call yogurt!

Samson's strength was in his hair. When Delilah deceived him and cut his hair, he became a prisoner of the Philistines. The Philistines took him to their temple in Gaza in front of an assembly to ridicule him, little realizing that his hair had grown back. One wonders whether while in prison his main diet was yogurt. Just one cup of plain yogurt provides 8.3 grams of protein, 294 milligrams of calcium and 323 milligrams of potassium. Calcium and potassium are the minerals for muscular strength. Yogurt was a popular food during Bible days. Samson prayed and God restored his strength. That day when Samson pulled the supporting pillars of the temple, 3000 Philistines were killed.

My parents ate it all the time. I didn't. I never liked it. But then, in those 1935 Depression days there was not much to eat. And I was to discover later that Laban (or yogurt) provided real sustenance for my parents in this trying time.

The Weekly Ritual

Every week the making of the yogurt was a creative ritual at our house. Today all sorts of equipment is available for making yogurt; multiple-size bottles, thermometers, yogurt sets, etc.

My mother would simply take a large bowl, a plate to cover it and cheesecloth. She used a tablespoon of starter or activator (which is the culture of the bacteria *bulgaris*) to each 2½ cups of milk. The milk was brought to a boil. When the broth came to the top, she lowered the heat and let the milk simmer for 2 minutes. She then let the milk cool to a point where by dipping her finger in the milk she could count to ten and withstand the temperature. This was her thermometer. Any skin on the surface of the milk was removed.

She added a few tablespoons of hot milk to the activator, beating vigorously. Then she slowly added the rest of the milk, continually mixing. All this mixture was placed in a large covered bowl where it "set" for 8 hours. When it became a thick, creamy custard substance it was transferred to a cheesecloth-type bag and hung in a cool place for eventual consumption that week.

This was Laban. And no amount of coaxing could get me to eat it. Ugh!

Yogurt has a long and colorful history. It is safe to say that yogurt was a staple dish during Bible days.

It has sometimes been described as "Persian Milk". In Iran it is known as *mâst*. The Egyptians call it *laban zabadi*.

Yogurt and Longevity

Yogurt has always been used as a food. Persian tradition has it that an angel revealed to the prophet Abraham the method of preparing yogurt. Some say because Abraham ate yogurt he lived to the age of 175. This makes interesting reading but is without any substantiation.

The secret of making yogurt was considered a valuable asset. This "inheritance of information" was passed down from father to son. Yogurt was such an important part of the Arab life that by the 7th century A.D. the Arabs were considered the leading civilized nation in the world. Scholars from London and from Paris and other leading centers of education converged on Cairo to study at the University. The reason; a book titled The Great Explanation of the Power of the Elements and Medicine was published in 633 A.D. in Damascus and revolutionized the medical world. The book contained information given by leading physicians in the Middle East that included the benefits found in yogurt!

Dioscorides of Cilicia (40-90 A.D.), a Greek writer on medicine, and a famous physician, recommended yogurt as medicine for tuberculosis, the liver, stomach, blood, as well as infections in the nose, ears and uterus.

**Yogurt
for
Ulcers**

Galen (130-200 A.D.), a physician, said that yogurt was far more beneficial for a burning stomach than milk. And he was right, but he didn't know why. Actually, yogurt is far more easily digested than milk.

In the 16th century when the Emperor Francis the First became sick, court doctors could not get him better. Someone suggested a famous doctor in Constantinople who had a "secret" medicine. He was secured and with him came his own goats. He concocted his secret medicine with the help of the goat's milk. That medicine was yogurt!

The Emperor got better and since then Frenchmen have called yogurt:

Lait de la vie eternelle
(Milk of Eternal Life)

Many people including babies cannot digest whole milk adequately. The reason: they have either lost or have a diminished supply of the enzyme lactase, which performs the digestive action. However, yogurt changes the chemistry of the milk making the lactase enzyme unnecessary. This is why yogurt is a more acceptable food than milk for a majority of people.

**Yogurt
Surpasses
Milk**

Experiments show that only 32 per cent of milk consumed is digested within an hour; 91 per cent of yogurt is digested within the same period.

Ilya Metchnikoff, a Nobel prize winner of 1908, was amazed at the longevity of Bulgarian peasants. Metchnikoff was Professor of the Pasteur Institute. He found they consumed large quantities of yogurt.

**Yogurt
the Nearest
of a
Miracle Food**

There are many Russians families who live high in the mountains and are over 100 years old. One reason is that they eat plenty of yogurt. Yogurt, incidentally, is soured milk which has a wonderful lactic acid that aids in protein, calcium and iron assimilation.

It has been reported that Bulgaria has almost 1700 robust healthy people over 90 in every million population! The United States, on the other hand, has only 9 people over 90 in every million. Could the reason be their large consumption of yogurt?

Now, no one food can be considered a miracle food. But yogurt runs high on the list as a "must" food for most people. The ideal nourishment is a high intake of fresh, uncooked foods, grown in soil free of chemical poisons and artificial fertilizers. Food should be cooked only when necessary to break it down and make it digestible. And steaming is the preferred way to accomplish this.

Some people complain of getting gas when they eat yogurt. This is an indication that yogurt is doing its job as a peacemaker . . . bringing peace to an ill body . . . warning against unfriendly bacteria!

**The
Friendly
Bacteria**

You see, yogurt creates friendly bacteria. Both yogurt and acidophilus milk contain lactose or milk sugar. This is broken down into lactic acid in the intestine and it wages a very vigorous war against harmful bacteria. That gas you experience is an indication that the battle is going on in your behalf. It also shows you need this friendly assistance that yogurt can supply. Many nutritionists believe that yogurt is far better for solving indigestion than antacids or bicarbonate of soda.

They also believe yogurt is excellent for relieving constipation.

Chasing out the "Blackhats"

Now to get back to the lactose in yogurt. Lactose is not digested until it reaches the intestines. Absorption takes place in the colon. The minerals in the yogurt aid in this absorption. When this occurs the friendly bacteria . . . yogurt's natural peacemaking force . . . thrives and multiplies. They produce so many additional brothers and sisters that the "unfriendly blackhats" find it difficult to exist and go riding out into the sunset!

Modern day medicine uses antibiotic pills and injections such as penicillin and the tetracyclines to get rid of intestinal infections. But these medicines destroy the good guys as well, the normal and necessary microbial intestinal flora.

This causes what is called avitaminosis. The word, *avitaminosis*, means literally, <u>without vitamins!</u> And the reason the body finds itself without vitamins is because the antibiotics destroy the friendly intestinal flora.

Getting Rid of "Travel Tummy"

"Travel tummy" from which most tourists suffer when travelling in the Middle East could be due to a lack of *lactobacillus acidophilli*, which is the friendly bacteria that is present in yogurt. The people in the Middle and Far East do not appear to be bothered by the same food, for their diet includes yogurt. And while Israel and the Arab nations cannot seem to end their wars, at least their collective "tummies" seem to be at peace because they daily ingest the friendly bacteria found in yogurt.

The digestive juices in the stomach are acid. The protein that we take in daily can only be digested in an acid medium. As people grow older their stomachs tend to lack a sufficient quantity of hydrochloric acid. They begin to have difficulty in digesting meats, nuts and cheese. It makes good sense to eat yogurt as yogurt aids the process of digesting proteins.

Yogurt and the Elderly

In the 1930's and 1940's many medical journals praised the use of yogurt for correction of gastrointestinal disorders. It was found superior to standard prescription recommendations in the treatment of children with infantile diarrhea. Some doctors have even used yogurt in treating vaginal infections.

Yogurt has been used in the treatment of stomach ulcers, gallbladder disease, gas, colitis and constipation. And yogurt has been used with cancer patients.

In our sophisticated world it seems easier to take an antibiotic either by pill or injection rather than eat yogurt regularly. Could we now be reaping the results in continued colds and a host of other infections, because we have successfully killed the friendly bacteria so necessary for sound, healthy bodies?

In the July, 1960 edition of Modern Nutrition, it was reported that one 8-ounce cup of yogurt has an antibiotic value equal to 14 penicillin units. Dr. William MacNider said:

The originator of lactic acid milk has

saved the lives of more children than the originator of Diptheria Antitoxin.

Lowers Cholesterol

Dr. George V. Mann, of the Vanderbilt University School of Medicine, conducted an experiment among the Masaia tribe in Africa. He reported in the American Journal of Clinical Nutrition, May, 1974, that something in yogurt reduces the blood levels of cholesterol.

Yogurt has a high acid content. It has a rather sharp taste. And it is not a taste that will generate swift acceptance by your family, particularly the youngsters.

My mother made yogurt fresh just about every week. But I stayed away from it as though it were some kind of poison.

The French may have been right when they called it "the milk of eternal life."

Certainly there are some evidences that a regular use of yogurt may contribute to a more healthy life, and consequently, longevity. It makes sense.

The Day I Discovered Yogurt

But it wasn't until one hot day, a very hot day, in New York (about 1975) that I first became acquainted with yogurt. Walking to the train station I saw a crowd around a store. Inquisitive, I walked by. They were all buying a new concoction called Frozen Yogurt.

I couldn't resist. I bought a vanilla-flavored cone. Surprised, I discovered it tastes almost like ice cream. I relished that frozen yogurt cone all the way to the train. At last, I was hooked on yogurt.

However, I soon discovered that yogurt has been victimized by the profitmakers. It is difficult to buy natural yogurt anymore. It has been loaded with sugar and messed up with fruits and preserves which add more sugar.

**Don't
Stir
the
Yogurt!**

What most people do not realize is that the minute you stir up the sugary fruits from the bottom of a yogurt container . . . you automatically destroy the *acidophilus*, the friendly bacteria that goes to work against the unfriendly bacteria! In effect, you are now simply getting about 8 grams of protein and some sugar.

Read the label on your yogurt container before you buy it. If it contains sugar, avoid it. Better to buy unflavored yogurt and eat it. Perhaps at first your taste buds will rebel. But remember, yogurt is a peacemaker. And soon those warring tastebuds will make peace with yogurt. And you will love it. It will tranquil your troubled tummy. It will bring calm to your churning colon and help make you a "regular fella."

It won't give you eternal life. But it may contribute in great measure to helping you enjoy life while you are here!

Yes, I can still remember that lazy summer day in Schultzille. I can still see that bag of Laban (yogurt) hanging from the door. And I still wonder what those butter fish would have tasted like.

If only that cat hadn't stolen my prize catch!

Well, I've made a greater discovery.

I've discovered yogurt! Isn't it about time you did too?

YOGURT BREAKFAST CEREAL
6 Servings

After you yawn, blend:
- **1 cup yogurt***
- **1/4 cup raisins**
- **1/4 cup chopped nuts**
- **1/2 cup oatmeal**
- **2 tablespoons orange juice**
- **1/2 cup sliced, drained peaches**
- **1/2 cup sliced apples**
- **1/2 cup sliced bananas**
- **1 tablespoon honey**

It is best first to blend the honey into the yogurt and then add the remaining ingredients. (You may wish to first soak raisins overnight. This soaking plumps the raisin and eliminates possible gas) Eat as you would any breakfast cereal.

YOGURT/CHEESE PIE
6 Servings

With great anticipation, prepare and cool:
- **9″ graham cracker pie shell***

In small saucepan, combine:
- **1/3 cup milk**
- **1 envelope unflavored gelatin**

Stir to soften gelatin. Warm over low heat, stirring constantly, until gelatin dissolves.

Combine in blender or bowl:

- **1 cup cottage cheese**
- **1 1/2 cups plain yogurt**
- **3 tablespoons honey**
- **dissolved gelatin mixture**

Whip briefly. Chill mixture 30 minutes until it begins to set. Pour into pie shell and chill.

Exotic options: (1) Put **1 cup of sliced bananas** into pie shell before pouring in yogurt mixture; (2) Instead of pouring filling into a pie shell, layer with **fruit** in parfait glasses.

*Graham Cracker Pie Crust
(Makes 1 pie crust)

Combine and press into 9″ pie pan:
- **1 1/3 cups graham cracker crumbs**
- **3 tablespoons honey**
- **1/4 cup melted margarine**
- **1/4 teaspoon nutmeg**

Bake at 375° for 8 minutes.

SPINACH and YOGURT SALAD
6 Servings

Take:
- **1 lb. fresh spinach**
- **(or 1/2 lb. frozen leaf spinach)**

and remove any tough stems, wash and drain. Chop the leaves. Stew them in their own juice in large, covered saucepan until leaves are tender. This should be about 15 minutes. (If using frozen spinach, defrost in colander, simmer till cooked) Allow to cool.

With vigor, beat:
- **1/2 cup yogurt**

with:
- **1 clove garlic crushed**

Add this mixture to the chopped spinach. Mix well and season with your favorite herb seasonings.

CUCUMBER and YOGURT SALAD
4 Servings

With joy and happiness, take:
- **1 large cucumber**

and dice it, leaving it in colander to drain for about 1/2 hour.

With zest, crush:
- **3 cloves garlic**

by first slicing and placing them on plate lightly sprinkled with garlic salt and then crushing.

Then mix:
- **4 tablespoons yogurt**

with the garlic, stirring well. Then add this mixture to:
- **2 cups yogurt**

Add salad seasoning to taste. Finally, to crown this salad, add:
- **1 tablespoon dried crushed mint (or 2 tablespoons finely chopped fresh mint)**

Now, drain the cucumbers and mix with the yogurt dressing. Pour into attractive serving dishes and top each dish with a sprig of fresh mint or parsley. Or go wild and dust lightly with cayenne pepper!

AUNT EFFIE . . .
Penelope wants to live forever!
Do you think raw oysters are healthy?

I never heard one complain! Live forever? I just found out
Penelope's husband was an undertaker. I thought you
told me he was a doctor.

> *No, Aunt Effie, I just said*
> *he followed the medical profession!*

Well, the way she's eating she certainly is not going to live
forever. She doesn't turn on the stove. She just lights up
the grease. Now I heard that Penelope's had plastic
surgery. Her husband took away all her credit cards. She
eats so much packaged junk foods that her garbage can is
loaded with tins and cartons. One day she ran after the
garbage man and said, *"Am I late for the garbage?"* He
said, *"No, jump in!"*

Between bad breath and a nagging vaginal infection,
Penelope better get acquainted with yogurt. Plain yogurt,
not that fancy, sugary, fruity stuff, can make her breath
kissing sweet and bring peace back into her family. It has
that friendly bacteria that will clear her colon and cleanse
her breath. And frequent applications of yogurt for early
vaginal infection will help that problem, too, for good!

7

OLIVE . . . THE OIL OF PROMISED HEALING

It is sad to see olive oil being replaced in our diets by the fancy, new hydrogenated, heat-pressed oils and margarines.

Margarine, as an example, is a completely artificial product. It is full of additives, chemicals and emulsifiers. Added to margarine are such chemicals as diacetyl, stearyl citrates and preservatives such as sodium benzoate or benzoic acid. The oil is hydrogenated, which means "hardened" and this process destroys the valuable lecithin which is nature's cholesterol fighter.

Avoid Commercial Shortenings

Commercial shortenings are hydrogenated as well and should be avoided. Old fashioned lard comes from pork. It is a saturated fat and should be avoided. Cottonseed oil and coconut oils should be avoided. Cottonseed oil is loaded with pesticides. Coconut oil is very high in saturated fats.

Most oils purchased in a health food store are acceptable; such as corn oil, sesame oil, safflower oil or peanut oil. In my opinion, the king of oils is OLIVE OIL.

When Noah was 480 years old, God revealed to him that he should build an ark (Genesis 6:14). For 120 years Noah and his family labored in constructing an ark 450 feet long, 75 feet wide and 45 feet high. It had never rained before! One can imagine the ridicule Noah faced in his community, building an ark on dry land for 120 years, and telling people there would be a flood. No doubt he was labeled both a quack and a fraud. But the rains came for 40 days and nights and the water covered the earth for 150 days. When Noah released a dove and it returned with an olive leaf, Noah knew God's judgment was over. In today's world, nutritionists attempting to guide people to sound nutrition, sometimes feel like a Noah in the midst of a doctor and drug-oriented society.

The best olive oil is that which is marked "Genuine Imported Virgin Oil."

Mineral oil should <u>never</u> be consumed. You will find it listed as an ingredient on many products. Be careful. Mineral oil interferes with vitamin absorption in the body.

Throughout history the olive tree has been acknowledged as a very special tree and its fruit, the olive pressed into an oil, a very special oil! The olive goes all the way back to the time of Noah. The first book of the Bible, Genesis, mentions in Genesis 8:11 how, after months on the water, Noah released a dove to see if there was any evidence of land.

> And the dove came to him toward evening; and behold, in her beak was a freshly picked olive leaf. So Noah knew that the water was abated from the earth.

And the last book of the Bible, Revelation, also mentions the olive in Revelation 11:4.

> These are the two olive trees and the two lampstands that stand before the Lord of the earth.

The two olive trees are references, in this verse, to the Two Witnesses (possibly Moses and Elijah) who are given supernatural power by God during the Tribulation Period to slay their enemies, to cause a drought, to turn water into blood, and to inflict plagues on those who have sown evil on the earth.

And throughout the Bible, the olive tree and olive oil hold a prominent place. If the Bible places this much favorable importance on the olive . . . from Genesis to Revelation; it is most reasonable to assume that the oil of the olive should be one of our highest priorities in the food we consume!

**The
Oil of
Healing**

The olive has always been portrayed with blessings and with healings. And while many learned doctors may feel the olive has no healing virtues, I personally believe that olive oil, as the Lord directs, can very definitely heal.

Sometimes we get so mysticized by the mechanics of medicine; the awesome and sometimes exasperating wait in the doctor's waiting room, the white coat and expensive equipment and array of pills, the impressive

but unreadable prescription, and the medicine with its long, difficult-to-pronounce name . . . that we automatically believe that anything that complicated and official looking just has to be good for our physical ailment. We don't want to be bothered to read the long list of side effects. Nor are we inclined to change our life-style, to benefit our physical condition.

Then, for someone to say that pure olive oil plus faith coupled with prayer can heal you . . . why something so simple, so austere, *"just has to be pure fraud and quackery."*

Bible Guidelines For Healing

In the New Testament in James 5:14-15, believers are given very specific directions on what to do when illness occurs:

> *Is anyone among you sick?*
> *Let him call for*
> *the elders of the church,*
> *and let them pray over him,*
> *annointing him with oil*
> *in the name of the Lord;*
>
> *and the prayer offered in faith*
> *will restore the one who is sick,*
> *and the Lord will raise him up,*
> *and if he has committed sins,*
> *they will be forgiven him.*

Now there are several things to observe in this promise from the Bible.

1. This promise extends only to believers.

2. The elders of the church are commanded to come and pray with the individual who is sick.

3. The individual, in praying, should confess any sins that he has committed.

4. The elders should annoint with oil in the name of the Lord.

5. The promise is that the Lord will raise him up.

As I have said many times, healing cannot be segregated to one phase of our being. Body, soul and spirit must work in perfect harmony for perfect healing! If you have a bitter spirit, and if your soul is not in tune with God, you may take a drug and outwardly feel better. But it is only temporary. Full healing comes when you confess your sins, right wrongs, acknowledge the Saviour and fuel your body with food that will help it and not hinder it!

The Carrier of Faith

The olive oil in itself does not actually do the healing. The olive oil is, so to speak, the "carrier of faith," the act of faith. This act of faith generates the spark and the healing is accomplished by God through the Holy Spirit. This is true Divine healing.

Many evangelical churches have shied away from anointing and having their elders visit the sick because of the overemphasis placed on healing by some Charismatics.

It is time for Bible-believing churches to recognize that James 5:14-15 is indeed a part of the Bible and a guideline that should be followed faithfully. Too often, Pastors themselves are the worst offenders of their body. They fail to recognize that it is the temple of the Holy Spirit. And when their body rebels, they seek out medical advice almost with religious fervor. As the leader of their church, they should first try God's way and encourage their members to, as well.

The olive tree was so important in the days of Moses that he exempted from military service men who would work at its cultivation. Olive oil was considered the oil of the eternal light (Leviticus 24:1-2).

To Anoint Kings

The olive was one of the "blessings" of the Promised Land. It was olive oil that was used to anoint kings (2 Kings 9:6). Oddly enough, you may think there is nothing beautiful about an olive tree. My wife and I have been to Israel several times and always go to the Garden of Gethsemane. There are several olive trees there; some perhaps, whose original stock go back to the time of Christ. The trees are gnarled with a grey-twisting trunks. Yet in the Old Testament book of Hosea we are told:

> *His beauty shall be like the Olive tree.*
> (Hosea 14:6 NAS)

And the beauty of the olive tree is in the life-giving oil its fruit will give when it is crushed. (This virgin oil of the first cold pressing is the only oil recommended.) As mentioned previously it is identified as virgin oil.

The olive oil does have natural healing properties when applied to the skin. The Good Samaritan in Luke 10:34 used olive oil to treat the wounds of a man waylaid by robbers.

Zechariah 4:12 refers to olive oil as ". . . the

golden oil." Those whose lives are productive and dedicated to the Lord are called ". . . *a green olive tree . . . of goodly fruit*" (Romans 11:17).

It is interesting to note that an olive tree will grow where no other tree can grow! And it will yield heavily with the minimum of care and culture. And quite oddly, olive trees are not bothered by bugs or other diseases common in the Middle East.

The Secret of the Olive

For every hundred flowers that blossom on the olive tree, only one in that hundred, produces an olive! This observation is even made in what some scholars believe is the oldest book in the Bible, Job, in Job 15:33!

Therefore, thousands of flowers on the olive tree never produce fruit. And the olive that is cultivated must be crushed to produce its "golden oil." What a lesson for all of us to benefit from!

The olive tree is found in abundance in Italy and Greece as well as in California. In the early days of Rome, olives were used as both the first course and the last course of their meals. During the reign of Scipio Africanus Major (234-183 B.C.), Roman citizens were given oil on a regular basis. So valuable was the oil to the citizen's well-being that Agrippa and Augustus followed this custom.

It was reported that the Roman ruler, Augustus (63 B.C. - 14 A.D.), when asking the poet and historian, Pollio, what ought to be done to preserve health in old age, was told:

Very little . . . rub yourself with oil.

While oil has been used in baths, its prime benefit comes from using it with our foods.

Olive oil has a very distinctive flavor. Those who have never tasted it sometimes allow their tastebuds to determine their preference for the popular tasteless, commercial oils.

How Olive Oil Gives Life to the Eggplant

Eggplant slices, when soaked in olive oil, suddenly come alive with flavor. As I mentioned before, one of my favorite dishes I enjoy during the summer months is barbecued eggplant. I don't know if it appears in any cookbook but my own. Perhaps I invented it.

I go out to my garden, pick an eggplant off the vine, and cut it in slices about 3/4″ thick. I then crush some garlic in olive oil (about 1 cup). The slices are saturated with this oil-garlic mixture and allowed to soak for several minutes. I then sprinkle some garlic powder and cayenne pepper on both sides of the slices.

This is placed on the barbecue grille, which has already been oiled with olive oil (to prevent sticking). In just a few minutes you have barbecued eggplant, charcoal browned and most delicious. In fact, this is making me so hungry, I think I'll do that tonight for supper!

In the Middle East, olive oil is a must for all cooking. In growing up, olive oil in our household was more in abundance than milk!

Olive oil should not be kept in the refrigerator because it tends to become semisolid. While it is cheaper to buy olive oil by the gallon, unless you store it properly in dark bottles and in a cool, dark place, it may become rancid.

The Dangerous French Fry Diet

We have a tendency to overheat our foods. French fries are one of the prime culprits in contributing to heart attacks. French fries are cooked in deep fat vats. The composition of the fat in the oils is <u>altered</u> when it is heated with the starchy french fries. It then becomes impossible for the liver to synthesize a perfect cholesterol from this oil for assimilation into the body.

The resulting cholestercl is then used by the body for arterial lining. Being an altered cholesterol, it does not function well. Soon it breaks down and is corroded. This results in various forms of arterial disease and degeneration. Hardening of the arteries you call it. Doctors call it arteriosclerosis!

A Natural Laxative

Olive oil promotes normal bile secretion and flow. Olive oil also has a natural laxative action. It aids in the healing of inflamed or injured skin.

It has been used by those who suffer from eczema and diabetes. Some have even taken an enema with olive oil. Some believe that the leaves from the olive tree lower blood pressure, promote urinary flow and drop blood sugar levels.

You might find it wise to adapt the eating habits of those in olive growing countries as far as salads are concerned. Most of them eat at least one salad daily. They drench the salad in olive oil and top it off with the juice of one-half of a lemon. From my observation it appears to be the lubricant that keeps things running smoothly for the digestion and assimilation of their food.

**The
Five-fold
Blessing**

I cannot think of a better lubricant for the human body than olive oil. Scripturally, it is compared to a promise (Noah), a blessing (Moses), a natural beauty (Hosea), an act in healing (James) and a symbol of righteousness (Revelation).

That's certainly not true of fast-fare restaurant hamburgers and french fries! They are dead foods!

That's why it's time we give olive oil a prime place in our daily diet. As Zechariah 4:12 reminds us, olive oil is the golden oil of productivity and life.

Why not choose life!

AUNT EFFIE . . .
Isn't Angus getting a little bald?

Better a bald head than no head at all! Besides his shiny dome lights up the night. It's good for those power blackouts we've been having. The moon casts a perfect glow on his dome. I know a couple who are so concerned with their health that whenever they have an argument the wife jogs home to mother. They say a woman's crowning glory is a rich man's scalp and Angus has done right with me!

Angus knows you can't cheat old father time. But some of the women drive a mighty close bargain with him. After all Angus is getting old. Old age isn't bad when you consider the alternative. There are three ages of man: youth, age and *"you are looking wonderful."* Angus is in that *"you are looking wonderful"* stage.

Of course, he could get more acquainted with the olive. It would certainly help his gout and stop his recurrent constipation. I've started to put olive oil in all my cooking and on my salads . . . none of that anemic, tasteless supermarket oil for me! I've even started massaging Angus' bald head with olive oil. If there is any hope in that scalp, olive oil will resurrect the hair! And olive oil mixed with grated garlic is an excellent liniment for joint pains, neuritis and sprains!

8

HOW TO COME ALIVE WITH A LEMON

**Ask For
Half a
Lemon**

I will always be thankful to Sunkist for making the lemon famous!

And to Dr. Carey Reams for making the lemon a most sought after fruit among nutritionists.

But, in my opinion, the lemon is still the most misunderstood fruit in the United States.

For a while lemons were "in." There was lemon shampoo, lemon soap, lemon shaving cream. And the citrus industry was kept busy. Suddenly the market dropped out on lemons and many planters removed or destroyed the lemon trees to make way for a more profitable crop.

The lemon is ill-treated. Ever go into a restaurant and order fish? When they bring the fish out to you, alongside is a micro-thin sliver of lemon . . . the juice of which wouldn't cover a thimble! And it usually looks like it has been recycled three or four times.

I shock the waitresses when I go to eat by asking them to bring me one-half a lemon. From past experience I find they don't understand such a request and still bring out a slice. Now, I am more descriptive! I tell them:

> Take a whole lemon . . . and with a knife cut it in half. Bring me one of those halves!

Next Time Try Lemon Juice

We are creatures of habit. We always drink orange juice for breakfast, and always load our broccoli with butter as well as our asparagus.

Why not squeeze a half a lemon into your orange juice in the morning?

"Oh," you say, *"but I've never done that before!"*

That's all right. Live dangerously. Try it. You'll like it! And that lemon will benefit you nutritiously! You'll find the lemon will give that orange juice a stimulating, tangy taste that will start the morning off right . . . get you moving forward!

How about that broccoli? Why drench it with butter. Instead soak it with the juice of a whole lemon! What an excellent flavor-aid and appetite-reviver that will bring zest into this otherwise normal dish!

You know, everytime I go out to a restaurant, I order asparagus. Why? So I can leave the waitress a tip!

Now that you're awake, let me tell you more about the marvelous lemon.

The Romans Had the Right Idea

The Roman poet, Virgil, revealed that among the richest productions of Media was a fruit he attributed the greatest virtues against all poisons! I am sure those who follow the Reams Lemon Water diet program will be pleased to learn this. Actually, there is nothing new under the sun. Not only Dr. Carey Reams[1], but many other nutritionists believe that the lemon aids the function of the liver in its detoxification of the poisons from the human body.

And So Did the Medes

And here the people of Media already recognized the value of the lemon 800 years before Christ! Media was located north of Persia and is now part of present-day Iran. Cyrus the Great in 556 B.C. formed the Medo-Persian empire. Quite possibly Esther, the Benjamite girl, who became Queen under King Xerxes, had lemons on the table of that fateful banquet with the schemer, Haman.

How did the lemon originate? The late A. J. Lorenz, who was director of nutrition research for Sunkist Growers, concluded that the earliest word from which "lemon" was finally derived meant "sour tree." I remember visiting a lifelong friend, Mrs. Charles Roth in Santa Ana, California, and picking a lemon from a tree in her backyard. It was so big that I thought it was an orange. And, while it had a tang, there was a sweetness there that I shall never forget!

The Chinese called the lemon "*i-mu*" because it was considered beneficial to a mother.

---

[1] Carey Reams is the nutritionist who practiced the highly controversial urine/saliva method of testing body chemistry. Among other things he believed that heart attacks can be foreseen years in advance — and prevented. He believed that most cancers are caused by a deficiency in minerals in one's body and that breast cancer can be avoided. **He is not a medical doctor. Health Guide For Survival** by Salem Kirban covers the story of Dr. Carey Reams and his urine/saliva theories. (It may be secured for $3.95 at your local bookstore or by writing: Salem Kirban, Inc., Kent Road, Huntingdon Valley, Pennsylvania 19006 U.S.A.)

Artists in the Middle Ages frequently pictured the child Jesus accepting an offering of a lemon. The lemon was an emblem of fidelity in love.

It is quite possible that lemons originated in India or China although it is interesting to note that lemons have been found to grow wild in the Middle Eastern countries.

The Golden Apple

The Greeks called the lemon the "golden apple."

Lemons were only known to the Romans at a very late period, comparatively speaking. At first the Romans only used lemons to keep moths from their garments. Quite an interesting use!

Pliny, the Roman naturalist and writer (23-79 A.D.) said that the lemon was an excellent counter-poison. Galen, the father of medicine, considered preserved lemon peel as one of the best digestive aids. It was often recommended for weak and delicate persons!

During the Middle Ages it was the custom to ban cold, moist fruit for infants. Yet paintings reveal that artists continued to show the child Jesus accepting offerings of it. In Christian symbolism, a lemon was not a fruit but rather an emblem of fidelity in love!

By the 4th Century B.C. lemons were grown by Italian gardeners. Much of these lovely gardens were destroyed by the Lombard invasion of 568 A.D.

One may not realize that no citrus fruits are native to the western hemisphere. The Crusaders were instrumental in the spread of the lemon and, later on, Christopher Columbus, on his second voyage in 1493, brought citrus seeds to Haiti.

Most all of us know how the orange and

lemon saved the English sailors. Voyages frequently began in early spring when most men, who had spent the winter on land, were in poor health. This was because of the months without fresh vegetables and fruits. A high proportion of the crew on these journeys became sick, many died. They were suffering from a Vitamin C deficiency disease known as scurvy.

**Lemons
a
Life Saver**

Their gums would swell, their flesh would remain indented when pushed in by one's finger. Wounds refused to heal. For 200 years physicians neglected the known remedy for scurvy, which was fresh citrus fruits. This to them was too expensive to give to sailors. They tried varied experiments to correct scurvy. None worked.

Finally, it was accepted that the juice of citrus fruits was the only medicine which could conquer a disease that was killing more seamen than enemy action. By the end of the 18th century, the British Admiralty decreed that a fixed amount of lemon juice should be issued daily to sailors in the British Navy. The mortality rate suddenly declined!

**The
Origin of
"Limeys"**

American sailors made fun of these English crewmen, sucking on lemons and limes. They began to taunt them and call them "limeys." Hence, the origin of that word. In the mid-nineteenth century English sailors started to switch to limes because they were cheaper. But they were also lower in Vitamin C and less effective. Finally, they reverted back to lemons.

**How
Lemons
Helped Me**

An interesting fact about the lemon tree is that the lemon produces blossoms, buds and mature fruit on the same tree at the same time! I have great respect for the lemon. My book, Health Guide for Survival,[1] covers in detail my rendezvous with the lemon and how the daily lemon-water drink benefited me nutritionally. At 51 I could feel myself going downhill physically. I thought it was a natural sign of old age. It was then I was introduced, via Dr. Carey Reams, to the lemon. He showed me how "when life gives you lemons . . . to make lemonade."

I can honestly say, after 2 years of following this nutrition program I feel great! At 53, I feel like 21!

Many believe, and I agree, that the lemon is the most valuable of all fruit for preserving health.

Those with ulcers usually cannot tolerate lemon in any form. Dr. Carey Reams, a biophysicist, has aided thousands of people through his former health retreats in Blue Ridge, Georgia; Roanoke, Virginia and his new retreat location at Murrietta Hot Springs in California.

It is his belief that lemon-water is beneficial for ulcers when used for just a very short time, a day or two, to remove the mucous covering that is protecting the ulcer. He has then recommended stopping the lemon-water liquid intake and substituting cabbage juice for its

[1] Salem Kirban, Health Guide for Survival
(Kent Road, Huntingdon Valley, Pennsylvania 19006; $3.95)

healing power with ulcers. To take the cabbage juice without removing this mucous covering does not allow the juice to reach the root of the problem.

Lemons Rich in Nutrients

Lemons are very rich in potassium, in Vitamin C, in calcium and also Vitamin A.

The lemon has been used as an astringent, as a drink for fevers, for rheumatism and as a counteraction against poisons.

The lemon peel has been known to be a stimulant of the appetite and also antibacterial because of its content in essential oil. Some people rub their teeth and gums with a lemon slice. They have found it to be an astringent with a hardening action on soft gums and also a whitening effect on the teeth.

How to Juice the Lemon

To get the greatest amount of juice from a lemon, roll the whole fruit on a hard surface, gently but firmly pressing it with the palm while rolling, before cutting for juicing.

This chapter took me two hours to write . . . and while writing it I drank the following:

10:00 AM	4 ounces of Lemon/Water combination
10:30	4 ounces of distilled water
11:00	4 ounces of Lemon/Water combination
11:30	4 ounces of distilled water

More details on the specifics of the lemon/water program are found in my book, How To Eat Your Way Back To Vibrant Health.[1]

Paul Natschowny at Hatfield Polytechnic,

---

[1] Salem Kirban, How To Eat Your Way Back to Vibrant Health (Kent Road, Huntingdon Valley, Pennsylvania 19006; $3.95)

Hertforshire, England, on February 19, 1975 ate 12 quarters (3 lemons) whole (including the skin and seeds) in 55 seconds; according to Guinness Book of World Records. While he broke a world record, such a consumption of lemons is highly inadvisable!

A Lemon Is Not a Car

Most people associate lemons with cars. I personally remember seeing a car going down the road painted all yellow with a big bright lemon on the door and a sign which read:

I bought this lemon from . . . . . .

and the name of the car dealer was prominently displayed.

This gives the lemon a bad name. Actually, the lemon is highly beneficial as a fruit and in a nutritional program.

It was Thomas Moore who wrote:

A Persian's heaven is easily made;
'Tis but black eyes and lemonade.

There is nothing like a cold glass of lemonade on a hot, humid day. In fact, it is an all-year refreshment. In the lemon you will find a gold mine of eating that will give spark and sparkle to your life.

Live It Up With a Lemon

It is carefully packaged by nature to add flavor with few calories. You can really live it up with a lemon when you generously saturate your vegetables with fresh (not reconstituted) lemon juice.

I've been living it up with the lemon for two years. And I've never regretted a day of it.

**Be as
Daring as
Columbus**

Remember, I told you that the Chinese highly valued the lemon as extremely beneficial for mothers. And all I can say is:
If it's good enough for mother,
IT'S GOOD ENOUGH FOR ME!

So, for tomorrow's breakfast, be as daring as Christopher Columbus and discover new vistas of life. Squeeze some lemon in your orange juice! Zing! Pow! Wow! Experience the thrill of living it up with a lemon!

FRIGE-CAKE LEMON CHIFFON   6 Servings

That's Frige like in refrigerator. The English call a <u>refrigerator</u> a *"frige."* They also call an elevator a *"lift."* And they call a bag, a *"sack."* And when one gets fired, he gets *"sacked."* And, if I don't get on with this recipe, I'll get sacked! Now I know why some restaurants have a Rainbow Room. When you eat there and get the check, your face turns all colors!

Anyhow, disturb your chickens and gather together:
   8 eggs
Now, do this with tender and understanding love (as I hate sad good-byes) ... <u>separate</u> (and with a lilt in your voice, sing *Should Auld Acquaintance Be Forgot*) the egg whites from their mother egg yolks. Place:

   **8 egg yolks
      in the top of a double boiler**
and to these lonely yolks, add:
   1 cup raw sugar[1]
   ⅔ cup freshly <u>squozed</u> lemon juice[2]
   ⅛ teaspoon sea salt[3]

Now, remember this is in a double boiler! Now heat the above over the <u>simmering</u> water, stirring, until mixture thickens.

Then, all by itself, take
   ¼ cup <u>cold</u> water,
and soak:
   2 tablespoons unflavored gelatin.
      Stir to dissolve gelatin, then add the gelatin/water mixture to the hot egg mixture. Now, allow this mixture to cool until liquid starts to thicken.
Beat with vigor:
   8 egg whites
      until stiff but not dry
And with the joy of a family reunion, fold:
   Egg whites into cooled mixture!
      along with
   1 teaspoon grated lemon rind
Pour mixture into well-buttered deep pie plate sprinkled with:
   ⅓ cup graham cracker crumbs on bottom and sides
Chill several hours in the "frige" before serving.

[1] *I hate to use sugar, you may wish to experiment with honey. Let me know how you make out.*

[2] *Squoze (as in squozed lemon juice) that's the plural of <u>squeezed</u>! (Only kidding, luv, no such word, but it makes the recipe come alive!)*

[3] *Sea salt can be left out. The sky won't fall down.*

LEEKY LEMON SOUP
6 Servings

You must be kidding! Leeky Lemon Soup? Come to think of it, I've seen a lot of leeky lemons. Every time someone across the table squeezes a lemon on his food, it springs into my eye! This recipe is so sacred it is guarded by 14 carrots and 1 stalk of celery! Well . . . here goes adventure!

Tell the kids to turn off the TV and go out and play. But first, stuff some carrot sticks in their hand. Then, bring to boil:

3 quarts chicken stock*

Chop and add:

1½ lbs. fresh leeks, including green tops
1½ lbs. carrots
1 stalk celery

Now add:

½ cup wild rice

Simmer for about 1 hour or just until vegetables are crisp, yet tender. Then, with great joy, add:

½ teaspoon summer savory
½ teaspoon marjoram
¼ teaspoon rosemary
2 tablespoons parsley, chopped
3 cloves slivered garlic
Juice of 1 lemon

Simmer for about 1/2 hour. Then, skim off the top and discard. Stir in:

Juice of 1 more lemon

Soup should have a tangy taste. If not, put in a little more lemon juice. Then serve.

* *If you do not have chicken stock, bring to boil **3 qts. water and 10 chicken bouillon cubes.** For greater hilarity and a tang of shocked surprise, in the last simmering cycle, sprinkle in some **cayenne pepper!***

LEMON SALAD SUPREME
4 Servings

I know, the first thing you are going to say is "Who ever heard of a Lemon Salad?" Correct! No one ever heard of one! So like, Columbus, let's see what we can discover!

Gather together, as a shepherd would gather his flock:

4 cups spinach leaves chopped
1 lb. raw string beans chopped
8 romaine leaves chopped

To this add, finely chopped:

2 tomatoes
1 cucumber
1 onion

Shower lavishly with:

Olive oil
Juice of 1 lemon
Herb seasonings

With delight of anticipation, serve into 4 bowls and top each bowl with:

2 slices lime
2 slices lemon*

* *Cut off the yellow peel from the lemon, leaving the white area (which is rich in bioflavonoids). And never, never serve a slice of lemon with seeds . . . so your guest can eat the whole slice, rejoicing!*

AUNT EFFIE . . .
Why is Percival's bile so vile?

I'd call it a case of aggravated assault. Suppose you had a wife who thought she was Teddy Roosevelt. Everytime she goes out she runs from store to store, yelling "CHARGE!"

Then, too, Percival came from a long line of writers. His sister wrote books that no one would read. His brother wrote songs that no one would sing. His mother wrote plays that no one would see. And his father wrote checks that no one would cash! And Percival's wife is on a sea-food diet. Every time she sees food, she eats. Percival is so doctor-oriented he gobbles pills like a famished chicken pecking up corn. He's reached middle age now . . . you know the time when what makes you tick needs winding. Percival's wife thinks she's Miss America. While it looks like she has a nice figure I happen to know it's only a bulge in a girdled cage!

Trouble with Percival is that his liver is not filtering all the poisons out of his system. His bile is supposed to help his digestion but he's got a clogged engine. Granny Osgood tells me she takes 4 ounces of lemon juice and mixes it with 36 ounces of distilled water. Then every hour for 8 hours a day she drinks 4 ounces of this lemon water combination. Gets her liver functioning, gives her energy, and makes her feel younger!

9

INVESTING IN NATURE'S LIQUID GOLD

**Carrots
Are For
People**

Carrots, when reduced to a liquid, are nature's liquid gold!

But, unfortunately, the carrot has been given a backseat in the eating habits of most people. Too many associate the carrot with rabbits. Rarely, except among nutritionists, are they thought of as a people food.

Many children develop a disdain for carrots ... such taste preferences usually imposed on them by their parents. And when carrots are cooked, they are generally cooked to death and made tasteless.

Perhaps that's why when carrots are served they are usually served as glazed carrots ... sweetened to death with a glaze that kills most of the nutritional benefit the individual would receive.

The carrot is a relative of the parsley family.

The carrot was well known to the ancients and is mentioned by Greek and Latin writers.

Pliny, the Roman naturalist, wrote:

> *The carrot begins to be fit for eating at*
> *the end of the year, but it is still better*
> *at the end of two.*

Carrots Have An Illustrious History

The name *Carota* for the garden carrot is found first in the writings in a book by Apicius Caelius (A.D. 230).

Apicius was a gourmet. He and his Roman friends loved to eat. However, when he discovered that he only had three-quarters of a ton of gold bullion left, he became despondent. You see, three-quarters of a ton of gold bullion in Roman days was only worth 1½ million dollars! And Apicius, being the gourmet that he was realized that it would be impossible to maintain his standard of living on this paltry sum. So he committed suicide!

Galen, the second century physician, added the name *Daucus* to distinguish the carrot from the parsnip, for which it was often confused.

In centuries past, carrots have been a mainstay vegetable throughout the world. In England they were first cultivated in the reign of Queen Elizabeth, having been introduced by the Flemings, who took refuge there from the persecutions of Philip II of Spain.

The Day Carrots Were Worn As Hats

Vegetables were rather scarce in England at that time and the carrot was welcomed with open arms. It became a general favorite. Even Shakespeare mentioned them in The Merry Wives of Windsor.

In the reign of James I, it became the fashion for ladies to use its feathery leaves in their headdresses! Perhaps this style will come back. That might prove a double benefit.

It was Sir Winston Churchill, who said in a press conference on May 25, 1943:

> *We shall continue to operate on the Italian donkey at both ends, with a carrot and with a stick.*

Carrots have long been alluded to as a prize. But the way most Americans shun carrots one would think they were a poison. The carrot has been bred in recent days to have a blunt end, so as to not perforate the polyethylene-shrouded bags.

The Power Packed Ounce

Carrots grow from tiny seeds. About 24,000 carrot seeds weigh only 1 ounce! The ancient Greeks and Romans used carrots for medicine but not for food.

Many alert people today are going back to the carrot to maintain or regain their health. Most medical doctors feel there is no redeeming qualities in drinking carrot juice. I would disagree.

A Doctor's Dim View of Carrots

In a recent newspaper article, a writer asked the physician-columnist if carrot juice was good for the body.

The doctor replied:

> *You hear some weird medical claims for various foods and juices. Celery and carrot juice are harmless . . . but they have no magical qualities . . . How do you "cleanse" the human system? If researchers found a way to do it, I doubt it would be through carrot and celery juice.*

Need a tranquilizer? Why not nibble on a carrot instead of crackers, cake or candy? Just one carrot supplies you with 15 milligrams of calcium, 140 milligrams of potassium and 4500 I.U. of Vitamin A. As an added bonus you get a cleansing roughage for your bowels.

**Carrots . . .
A Most
Perfect Food**

Yet, through the centuries, the humble carrot has been considered one of mankind's most valuable nutrients. It is considered by many as the most perfect food. It is extremely high in Vitamin A and potassium and rich in the B complex vitamins and other minerals.

Carrots should never be peeled. Rather, if needed, scrape them or brush them under running water as the skin is the richest and tastiest part. Russians have extracted from the carrot a chemical called *daucarine* which is a strong vasodilator of the coronary blood vessels.

**Rich In
Vitamin A**

Carrots are rich in alfa-beta-gamma carotene, which is responsible for its typical coloration. The beta-carotene, also called provitamin A, is transformed into Vitamin A when we eat the carrot. Vitamin A does not really exist, in the form we utilize it, in any vegetable. What we are eating (or drinking, in the case of carrot juice) is carotene. When our body assimilates it, the liver manufactures the true Vitamin A.

A vitamin A deficiency can reveal itself in many ways. One of them is dry skin. If one experiences difficulty in adjusting vision due to changes in intensity of light . . . like going into a dark room from a light one or night driving, with its various light changes; such could indicate a lack of Vitamin A. Dryness in the nose, mouth, throat or in the genital organs could also indicate a lack of sufficient Vitamin A.

Cavities or soft enamel on the teeth, sinus trouble, susceptibility to colds, and respiratory infections could well indicate a Vitamin A deficiency.

**Carrots
A Hedge
Against
Disease**

Gallbladder disturbances and liver disease can block proper utilization of Vitamin A.

The U.S. recommended daily allowance for Vitamin A is 500 I.U. Many nutritionists believe that 10,000 I.U. should be recommended for adults daily.

Because of the diabetic's unbalanced fat metabolism and elevated blood cholesterol, Vitamin A utilization is often impaired.

Since the vitamin is soluble in fat, as we grow older, our utilization of Vitamin A is diminished. The liver contains about 90% of the total Vitamin A in our body. And when our liver is malfunctioning, it reflects in our general health picture.

Nutritionists have found the carrot a most valuable food. They believe the carrot provides energy, combats anemia, promotes normal growth and stimulates the appetite.

**Promotes
Elimination**

The carrot has been called the "great friend of the intestine." The carrot promotes normal elimination while preventing diarrhea.

Carrots have an analgesic action as well, alleviating pain. Many have used carrots for problems associated with arthritis, kidney disease, atherosclerosis (loss of elasticity in arteries) and liver and gallbladder disease.

**The
Fountain
of Youth**

Carrots are considered the "Fountain of Youth" vegetable and many have found that carrots delay aging and wrinkling of the skin.

Ragnar-Berg, an early nutritionist with a scientific background, stated that the carrot:

. . . constitutes a powerful cleansing food. A large amount of carrot carbohydrate is one of the most effective means of changing the intestinal flora from a putrefactive to a non-putrefactive type.

The drinking of carrot juice has long been a habit of many who believe in "back to nature" nutrition.

However, Dr. Carey Reams[1], perhaps, more than anyone else has brought the lowly carrot back to popularity.

To most everyone who has followed his nutrition recommendations he either suggests a daily intake of carrot juice or a vegetable drink. Reams' nutritionists recommend carrot juice to anyone whose sugar reading is 5.49 or lower. (Based on the Reams scale of sugar measurement.)

Excellent In Times of Stress

A 5 ounce glass of pure carrot juice contains over 30,000 I.U. of Vitamin A. Because of today's stress-environment living, many progressive nutritionists now recommend this as a daily intake. Carrot juice is the most perfectly balanced vegetable juice available today. It is double dynamite:

1. It readily gives up its energy to the body.
2. It helps the body to release energy from the fat stores.

As in any vegetable drink, it should be consumed immediately upon making so as to capture all its nutrients.

Carrot juice is not recommended for those whose sugar readings are 5.50 or above on the Reams scale. In those cases, Reams' nutritionists recommend a vegetable drink (sometimes called Green Drink), which can be made from any edible green leaf.[1]

Eliminates Fatigue

I, personally, have found that carrot juice helps me eliminate fatigue. I drink a glass every morning about 10 AM and I could go through until suppertime without eating. Of course, every half hour I drink either distilled water or lemon water during the course of the day. But while writing a book, I generally have a breakfast cereal with sufficient protein value, a combination 8 ounce glass of carrot, celery, and pear juice and then sit down at the typewriter ... abounding in energy and ideas. I skip lunch while I am writing but occasionally will have a special Kirban tomato sandwich at 3 PM liberally sprinkled with cayenne pepper!

through winters that are not too cold and they can endure much summer heat.

The Secret In Buying Carrots

Carrots, as in most any other vegetable, should taste sweet when eaten or reduced to a juice. If they taste bitter, you can count on the fact that they were grown on mineral-poor soil. They will lack the complete nutrients your body needs!

I can remember the first day after our 3-day fast at the Reams' Blue Ridge, Georgia retreat. At the breakfast table was a 4 ounce glass of

---

[1] More details on the Reams' Carrot juice and Green Drink combinations can be found in How to Eat Your Way Back to Vibrant Health by Salem Kirban, pages 74 and 76. Huntingdon Valley, Pennsylvania 19006. $3.95.

carrot juice. I looked at it in horror! I had never before drunk carrot juice. At first my taste buds rebelled.

Re-train Your Tongue

Isn't it odd how we have trained our taste buds what to like. And, how unfortunate, that we train the taste buds to like things like chocolate cake, candy and mashed potatoes!

Well, I had quite a tongue re-training program to undergo in just 3 or 4 short days.

It wasn't too long before I actually relished the taste of carrot juice. And I noticed my fatigue disappearing and my energy abounding.

They say that heredity is what man believes in until his son begins to act like a delinquent. It was the Duke of Windsor who remarked in March, 1957:

> The thing that impresses me most about America is the way parents obey their children.

And this is more fact, than fiction. In fact, increasingly we are seeing even school principals knuckling down to the demands of their students.

Good Nutrition Begins at Breakfast

In my opinion, most students are ill-fed, who have as their breakfast such gastronomical fancies as "Coke and pretzels" or a sugary cereal that isn't fit for a sick dog. For snacks they ingest a candy bar or chocolate cupcake that has been imbeded in their mind by TV commercials as an *"energy break."*

Some children and parents as well are awakening to the fact that most of the health and mental problems youngsters face today is directly attributable to poor nutrition. They are throwing out the school vending machines that dispense soft drinks, candy and cookies, and putting in machines that dispense fresh fruits and fruit drinks.

I say, *"more power to them!"*

Will It Ever Happen? What a terrific drop we would see in school vandalism, which now amounts to over $600 million annually in the United States, if we would send our children to school with celery and carrot sticks to munch on!

Could it be that our children develop diseases of their parents because of the bad eating habits they pick up from their parents? I believe so!

Instead of holding out a carrot to a horse, as a reward ... isn't it time we started offering carrots to our youngsters (instead of money)? For money loses its value rapidly. But carrots? Ah! Carrots, my friend are nature's liquid gold!

CARROT STRING BEAN SOUP
4 Servings

With joy in your heart, grate gratifyingly:
  2 cups carrots
With care and precision, cut fine:
  2 cups string beans
  ½ cup celery including tops
  1 clove garlic
  1 tomato
Cover this combination with water and simmer 10 minutes. Season to taste with herb seasonings.

Kirban's
CARROT REVITALIZER SALAD
4 Servings

The night before (when not a creature is stirring . . . not even a mouse), sneak into the kitchen, awaken a generous handful of sleepy raisins and place them in a small bowl or container of water (preferably distilled water). Let them swim all night long and soak in the refreshing liquid.

Oh, yes . . . now you can go back to bed.

The next day, in a salad bowl (not you, the ingredients) combine:
  1 cup finely grated carrots
  ½ cup finely chopped string beans
  ½ cup finely grated raw young beets
  1 cup shredded romaine
  1 cup alfalfa sprouts
Now, mix these all together so they get acquainted. Then, hilariously throw in the plump, presoaked raisins and unite them with their friends.

Then grab a whole lemon. Tell him that you like him. And show him that you mean it by squeezing the juice out of the lemon into the salad. If you wish, season with herb seasonings.

P.S. If you want to live dangerously, when no one is looking, throw in **1/2 cup of chopped pecans!**

14 CARROT CAKE
8 Servings

With rich anticipation that you are concocting your own Ft. Knox, sneak over to the oven and preheat it to 350° F.
Then, take a large mixing bowl and with harmony in your heart, blend:
  1 cup honey
  1 cup oil
  4 eggs
Gradually add:
  2 cups unbleached flour
  ½ teaspoon baking soda
  2 teaspoons baking powder
and beat these well with all vim and vigor. Think of your pet gripe as you are beating. It will relieve your inner tensions.

Now, with renewed peace in your heart, add:
  1 teaspoon vanilla
  1 cup grated carrots*
  1 cup raisins
  1 cup chopped pecans
and mix thoroughly.
Take all this bundle of joy and bake it in an oiled and floured tube pan at 350° for 1 hour.
* *If you adore jewelry, you will have to select small, baby carrots in order to have a 14 Carrot Cake.*

CARROT HORS D'OEUVRE

Hors d'oeuvre means "outside the main works." Very simply an hors d'oeuvre is a taste-tempter, a palate tickler that prepares the guest for the good things to come at the main meal.

With an inner peace and calm, gently slice thinly:
  Carrots
Marinate these thin slices in:
  Lemon juice, freshly squeezed
  A touch of honey
Try and use baby carrots or thin sliced carrot sticks. Make enough for all your guests. And color with a sprig or two of parsley . . . then, afterwards, be sure to eat the parsley!

AUNT EFFIE . . .
Uncle Bromley's vision is failing and he complains that he is always tired.

Ain't no wonder. Imagine him partying all night playing post office. Why there ain't one of them Bromley clan that has sufficient postage! Uncle Bromley calls his wife, Echo. She always has the last word. No wonder Uncle Bromley is fatigued. He just celebrated his Tin Anniversary . . . 12 years eating out of cans. Uncle Bromley was telling me that he came home last night and found his wife's car in the dining room. "How did you get your car in the dining room?" he asked little Miss Echo. *"It was easy,"* she said, *"I made a left turn when I came out of the kitchen."*

I remember Granny Osgood was going blind with cataracts. She started drinking 6 ounces of carrot juice twice a day. And not only are her cataracts gone but she has more energy than I do. Then her niece's baby, Marigold, got all colicky and had trouble eating. Nothing seemed to suit the little tyke. Granny brewed up a carrot soup and it not only started Marigold eating but cleared up her diarrhea!

With the price of gas up so high, Uncle Bromley must have a fortune tied up in internal gas. Carrot juice will dispel that in a hurry! His engine will run better without gas!

10

MILLET . . . The Mistletoe of Vegetables

Why do I call Millet, the mistletoe of vegetables?

Building Energy Fast

The old custom of standing under the mistletoe is one that we all can recall. Standing under the mistletoe is an invitation to be kissed. And what vibrant energy ensues after that episode!

So with millet. Millet is an energy building food.

I can remember when I spent 10 days in March, 1976 at the Blue Ridge, Georgia retreat of Dr. Carey Reams. It seemed for almost every breakfast, after my fast, we had millet. But I learned to like millet. And Dr. Reams had a real reason for including it in the diet. It is full of nutrition and generates stamina. It's a stick-to-your-ribs breakfast!

Millet is a cereal grass whose latin name is *Panicum miliaceum*. Millet is so called because of its multiplicity of seeds.

One of the properties of millet is its fantastic ability to swell when cooked with liquids. Pliny, the Roman naturalist (23-79 A.D.), said that 60 pounds of bread could be obtained from a single bushel of millet, weighing only 20 pounds! That's some harvest. Modern day bakers should take a tip from this. Their profit picture may soar and the health of their customers, as well!

A Blessing To Millions

Almost one-third of the people of the world depend on millet for grain feeds and flours! In fact, in Japan, over 50 million bushels of millet seed are ground into flour each year. Unfortunately, in the United States most millet is grown to feed livestock and poultry; little of it finds its way to the dinner table!

Upper class Romans took a bath before banqueting. Their hands and feet were washed at the table by slaves. Besides millet, included in their banquet was salads, olives, pickled radishes, a few grasshoppers (french fried) and multiple courses, each heralded by a blast on the trumpets. After music and sensuous dances, the banquet was capped by a duel to death of several gladiators.

Panic Grass is a type of millet. It was preferred by the people of Greece and Turkey. The higher classes of Rome and Athens resisted this dish.

More Valued Than Gold

So important were these grains to the Greeks and Romans that anyone who set fire to his neighbor's grain field was punished by death. On top of that, they had special magistrates whose sole duty was to watch over the growing of the grain. And to this were added public distributors to prevent anyone from purchasing a greater quantity than was actually necessary for his wants!

The Roman government was so convinced that abundance of bread was one of the best means of maintaining public tranquility that they carefully rationed the millet-based bread and even gave loaves free to those who could not afford it.

Julius Caesar distributed bread to 320,000 plebeians (members of the ancient Roman lower class).

And, as you can expect, the Romans had an annual feast in honor of millet and other cereals. Every April 7th they celebrated the Feast of Ceres. Ceres was the Roman goddess of crops. The ladies of Rome dressed in white, flowing gowns, holding blazing torches. Millet cakes sprinkled with salt, honey, milk and wine were offered to the goddess Ceres. Pigs were sacrificed to her.

By 27 B.C. there were 329 public bakeries in Rome and many slaves had as their sole occupation that of making bread. They were so valuable that these slaves brought an exorbi-

The Romans Used Bran

tant price when sold. The Romans thought much of millet for their leaven. They mixed it with sweet wine, then let it ferment a year. They also used wheat bran and you thought bran was a new 20th century discovery!

The bakeries were quite ingenious and their bread was very decorative and eye-appealing.

The Manna From Heaven

In the Bible, millet is only mentioned in Ezekiel 4:9, where it was made into a bread during a famine. It may also be the pannag that is mentioned in Ezekiel 27:17. You remember when Moses and the Israelites fled Egypt that the Lord provided them with food that fell down from Heaven, coming down like rain (Exodus 16:14-16; Psalm 78:24). That food was called manna.

The word, manna, is a transliteration of two Hebrew words meaning:

What is it?

And that's exactly what I exclaimed as I sat down to a breakfast bowl of millet! WHAT IS IT? I asked my associate, Bob Conner. And, Bible scholar that he is, he still did not know!

Some believe that the manna that fell from heaven that day was millet. But that is opinion, not fact. One benefit of millet is its remarkable ability to expand, as we mentioned previously. And, perhaps the manna was some form of millet. Others believe it was coriander seed, a member of the parsley family. Anyway, we do know, like millet, it had the ability to provide nutritional substance that would carry one through the entire day!

Millet was generally used in the Middle East as "prison-fare" because it was unappetizing. It was unappetizing because they did not know how to properly prepare this vital food.

Very, very few cookbooks have any recipes on how to use millet. Yet millet can be used in bread, as a breakfast cereal, in casseroles, with lentil dishes, stuffed peppers and other vegetables and soufflés.

Rich In Minerals

One of the best ways to utilize millet is as a breakfast cereal. Millet seeds, estimated to be about 1500 years old, have been sprouted and they produced buds! Think of this stored up energy ready to burst into usefulness when you eat it! Millet is rich in protein, phosphorus, iron and the B vitamins.

The early Chinese made thin pancakes of millet meal. The Romans made a porridge of millet. Unleavened bread is the only kind you can make of millet flour, if used, use this flour exclusively. Millet flour lacks gluten and therefore does not rise.

The next time you sit down to a bowl of cereal and exclaim

WHAT IS IT?

It could be millet!

And if you go through the entire day on cloud nine abounding with energy, chances are you did have a breakfast rendezvous with the mistletoe of vegetables!

GOOD MORNING
MILLET CEREAL
4-6 Servings

Millet, like oats and barley, must be presoaked before cooking. It is best to soak overnight. Here is the secret to cooking millet as a breakfast cereal:

1. Start with rapidly boiling water.
2. Slowly add millet so that water keeps boiling. This allows each individual grain to be surrounded by hot water and thus, quickly penetrated.
3. The boiling point of the water must be maintained throughout as the cereal is added.

Following this procedure you will not have "gummy" millet ... as the boiling water allows the outer starch layers to stabilize and keeps the granules separated after swelling. The cereal is done when it is translucent.

Millet increases in bulk. You can count on 4-6 servings for each cup of uncooked cereal.
Take:
  1 quart water and bring to rapid boil
Slowly trickle in, while maintaining boiling,
  1 cup presoaked millet
Cover and let simmer for about 45 minutes or until millet is soft and translucent.
Add:
  1 cup raisins
  1 cup chopped, unpeeled cored apples
Cook 15 minutes longer. Serve with a dash of **honey** or **blackstrap molasses** and **milk** or **cream** as desired.

MILLET CASSEROLE
6 Servings

While the oven isn't looking, softly sneak over to it and preheat it to 350°.

Now, find a dry, heavy casserole and place in it:
  1 cup whole hulled millet
Place this <u>dry</u> millet in the casserole over a low heat so it browns slowly. After millet browns, <u>remove</u> it from casserole. What do I do with it now? Well, one thing sure, don't put it in your pocket! Just set the millet in another container. Got that? OK, now, take the empty casserole and to it, add:
  2 tablespoons oil
  2 onions chopped
Sauté onions until lightly browned. Now, for the grand reunion! <u>Return</u> millet to the casserole to get acquainted with the onions and also add:
  1 carrot chopped
  1 teaspoon sea salt
  A dash of cayenne pepper
    (if you're not chicken, that is!)
Pour over this glorious mixture:
  1 quart chicken broth*
  or beef broth
Now, put a lid on the casserole so that it is tightly covered and bake for 1½ hours or until millet is tender. How can you tell when the millet is tender? Ask it! When the millet is fully cooked it will look like rice with each grain separate. For greater delightful eating, stir in:
  1 cup sour cream
and top with:
  1 cup sliced mushrooms
This is such a substantial meal it can be served as the main dish.
* *If you do not have chicken broth, bring to boil 1 quart of water and 5 chicken bouillon cubes.*

MILLET MIDDLE EAST STEW
4 Servings

Be ready to sample the delights of exotic Arab lands by taking:

1 tablespoon olive oil*
½ lb. lamb cubed
½ cup onion chopped

and sauté in adequate saucepan. (I say, "adequate" because later in the recipe you will be adding 4½ cups water.)
Then, add:

1 cup zucchini squash
(cubed in ½ inch cubes)

and cook this combination 5 minutes longer. Now, add:

1 cup whole hulled millet
4½ cups water
1 tablespoon herb
seasonings

Bring to a boil, then cover and boil for 45 minutes. Stir to mix and let stand 10 minutes before serving.

* If you wish, you may substitute 1 tablespoon sesame oil. Then you can say "Open Sesame."
For greater tang, throw in some crushed **garlic** in the last 10 minutes and . . . just before serving, sprinkle with the **juice of one lemon.** I don't know how all this is going to taste . . . but it sounds good. Let me know how you make out and if you have any exotic suggestions to make this stew more taste-tempting!

AUNT EFFIE . . .
Agatha seems so forgetful lately!

Who can blame Agatha in this crazy mixed-up, complicated world. When you write a letter you gotta remember a 5-digit zip code for every town you write to . . . when you make a long distance phone call you gotta remember 11 numbers! Then there's a Blue Cross number, a Social Security number and a credit card number! And poor Agatha can't find a green spot on earth to walk on! Why the national flower in the U.S. should be a concrete cloverleaf!

For physical food, we eat plastic bread. For spiritual food when we have problems, we are fed Valium. No wonder she's forgetful. Agatha's body wasn't made to subsist on plastic and chemicals and to ingest polluted water and breathe polluted air. And those breakfast cereals . . . Old Kellogg would drog a "g" in his name if he could see the sugary samples they're putting out today as a "Good morning" breakfast. Sounds more like a "Goodbye" breakfast to me!

To get that memory back, Agatha needs a complete nutritional overhaul. She's got to start eating a bowl of millet in the morning and taking at least 800 I.U. of Vitamin E daily and a 6 ounce glass of fresh carrot juice mixed with celery juice about 10 AM daily. Then, she might remember more than she wants to!

11

HOW TO LIVE IT UP WITH A LENTIL

A
Forgotten
Food

Most Americans would not know a lentil if their life depended on it!

The lowly lentil is one of those forgotten foods that has been pushed aside for hamburgers and french fries.

Some may be surprised to know that just one serving of lentils has

7.8	grams of protein
19.	grams of carbohydrate
2.	milligrams of iron
250	milligrams of potassium
	plus a good amount of B vitamins and virtually no fat

Many health books that give food values of nutritious foods for some reason omit lentils. Lentils are called legumes. Legume means "anything that can be gathered." Other legumes include peas and beans. Actually, lentils are considered a part of the bean family.

Although the way things look, they appear to be in the "has-bean" family.

Lentils have been called the "poor man's

meat" because they are so low in cost, so easy to prepare, and so substantial a meal.

An Excellent Breakfast Food

From infancy on up, the Egyptians fed their children a generous supply of lentils. Actually in the Middle East countries lentils are consumed for breakfast, like you and I would eat a breakfast cereal. I might add, those who thrive on lentils do not get the mid-morning let-down like those those who have tea and toast, a soft drink and a pretzel, or coffee and a doughnut!

The Greeks highly esteemed the lentil. It was the hamburger of the Greek Age. Zeno, a Greek philosopher said:

> A wise man acts always with reason,
> and prepares his lentils himself.

He would never let anyone cook his lentils. He prepared this heavenly concoction with a passion beyond words.

And, of course, the Hebrews knew the value of this lowly legume!

If you recall Bible history, you remember Rebecca, the wife of Isaac, had twins, Esau and Jacob. Esau was the older one, having been delivered first. Esau grew up to be an outdoor man. He enjoyed hunting. Often he brought venison home to his father and became his father's favorite son.

On the other hand, Jacob won the favor of his mother.

Anyone who has been in the Middle East knows that even in the winter season it can be very hot . . . and temperatures can range well over the 100 mark.

Jacob means *supplanter* (to take the place of). Not only did he persuade Esau to sell him his birthright for a dish of lentils but he also fooled his father, Isaac, by pretending he was Esau. He may have met his match in Laban, his uncle. In courting Laban's daughter, Rachel, he was tricked into marrying Leah first.

**The Food
For Which
Esau
Sold His
Birthright**

One day Jacob cooked some savory dish which we now know as lentils. The Bible records this event in Genesis 25:29-32:

> And when Jacob had cooked stew,
> Esau came in from the field and he
>   was famished;
> And Esau said to Jacob,
>   Please let me have a swallow
>   of that red stuff there,
>   for I am famished;
> But Jacob said:
>   First, sell me your birthright.
> And Esau said,
>   Behold, I am about to die; so
>   of what use then is the
>   birthright to me?

Without getting into the spiritual connotations of these verses (and there are very important spiritual lessons here), there are some doctors who suggest that perhaps Esau was suffering from low blood sugar (hypoglycemia). It is not unusual for someone with hypoglycemia to become frantic for food, when they are weak. I know of one case where a wife beat on her husband's chest almost hysterically when her need for food became acute. Extreme hunger, fatigue, weakness, confusion are all symptoms of low blood sugar.

The birthright was a cherished legacy. This ancient custom meant that the family name and titles passed through the line of the eldest son. It not only entailed family inheritance but spiritual position in the family.

Esau, upon seeing this pot of lentils undoubtedly could also smell its delectable aroma afar off. For it is usually made with olive oil and smothered with onions.

Compelling Aroma

The heat of the day, the lack of food during hunting, could have left Esau at the point of complete prostration. The protein-rich lentil soup or stew was just exactly what Esau needed . . . "that red stuff." Lentils are small circular beans, almost flat and generally less than one-quarter of an inch in circumference. There are red and green varieties.

In such a state of confusion and famished one can understand how he would trade his most precious possession, his birthright, for food.

Esau may be the first recorded case of hypoglycemia. And without any medical background, he knew how to alleviate it.

This is not to say that we have any positive indication that Esau traded his birthright because of his hypoglycemic condition. The Bible does not say this. However, I pass it on as an interesting medical observation by some physicians.

The important fact is this: Esau valued lentils enough that he was willing to give up his spiritual and material inheritance . . . for just one bowl of lentils!

Lentils are referred to in 2 Samuel 17:28 when three farmers brought food to David and his men when they were hungry. In 2 Samuel 23:11, the Philistines were gathered together at a field of lentils, where Eleazar defeated them.

**Lentils
A
Life Saver**

And, in Ezekiel 4:9, Ezekiel commanded his people to take lentils along with millet and other beans and make bread to withstand the siege of Jerusalem. The siege was to last 1½ years! The people were rationed 10 ounces of bread a day and just 8 ounces of water daily!

The Romans weren't too emotional about lentils . . . although they loved to eat! They preferred to eat eels and snails. According to them, the moisture in lentils could only cause heaviness to the mind and render men reserved, indolent and lazy. Actually, lentils derives its origin from the word lentus which means "slow."

Actually the Romans used the lentil for food for funerals. And Marcus Crassus, a Roman general (112-53 B.C.) had great disdain for lentils. He was quite a character, himself. He could be considered the first Roman who "made a million dollars in real estate." Crassus acquired hundreds of houses and tenements in Rome and charged high rentals. Soon his fortune rose to over $25 million! Having become the wealthiest man in Rome, he was still unhappy; he wanted public office that brought fame and recognition!

He was known to remark:

No man should consider himself rich
unless he could raise, equip
and maintain his own army.

And that he did!

He raised a great army and led them against the Parthians. When his supply of corn became exhausted he was convinced that he

would be defeated because his men were
obliged to have recourse to lentils

**Don't
Disparage
The Lentil**

What a nasty thing to say about the lentil . . .
that it would bring defeat! But it was true!
General Marcus Licinius Crassus was defeated by the Parthians. The Parthian general,
nice man that he was, invited Crassus to
lunch with him. Crassus went and was bar-
barously slain; his head was cut off and the
head was used in a Parthian play in their
court the next day!

Perhaps that should be a warning to those
who would look down on the lowly lentil!

**An
Excellent
Protein**

There are some who believe that lentils are
hard to digest. The carbohydrates in lentils
consist mainly of pentosans and galactans.
Now, what in the world is a pentosan and a
galactan. They sound like a zoo animal to me.
Pentosan is a group of plant carbohydrates.
Galactan is white, crystalline sugar. Some believe that the presence of these two carbohydrates prevent the digestive enzymes from
penetrating easily and finally break up in the
large intestine (colon), causing gas (flatulence).

Actually, when properly prepared, lentils are
both nutritious and easily digestible. In the
Middle East, mothers find that they increase
milk production when they are lactating.

And that is the rub . . . proper preparation.

I can remember my mother and my Aunt
Wadia in our little home in Schultzville,
Pennsylvania, preparing lentils. They would
soak the lentils in cold water overnight so

**How To
Prepare
Lentils**

that the moisture would soften them. Then they would scoop up about half a handful of lentils and rub them together between their fingers removing the outer husk. They would keep doing this until the entire bowl was "worked over." They would also remove any lentils that floated to the top as these were undesirable because of mold or imperfections. The lentils were then ready for use, in a stew, in a soup or as a dish with olive oil and onions.

Lentils have been treated as second-class citizens in many current health food books as an incomplete protein. Nothing could be further from the truth! Lentils are a first-class protein. I find it odd that many scholarly medical and nursing books on nutrition don't even include the lentil as a food. I would not want to wish them the fate of General Marcus Crassus!

No food consists entirely of proteins. There is not a shadow of doubt that lentils are highly nutritious. Lentils consist of 12.35 percent water, 25.70 percent protein, 1.90 percent fat and 53.30 percent carboyhydrate. The balance are minerals. One can see that lentils have more protein than meat. And the mineral matter in lentils is higher than in any flesh food, fish or poultry.

The British do no use lentils much. However the people of Scotland do for they know good cheap food when they see it!

Although lentils do not contain the full balance of amino acids needed for the body, by including a few egg slices or three table-

Good For Hypoglycemics

spoons of yogurt you will have a complete protein meal. Lentils have as their basic benefit protein-value, a food that provides endurance and stamina . . . a food hypoglycemics would welcome.

The smaller red lentils are richer in protein than the large.

Lentils are one of the few vegetables that can be grown with little nitrogen requirements. This has made lentils an easy crop to raise in India and the Middle East.

Every Friday while I lived at home, my mother would make lentils. You could count on it for lunch or dinner. And I always looked forward to that meal.

When I got married, my mother and then my father (after she passed on) would always have a dish of lentils waiting for me on Sundays when we stopped at their house on the way back from church. The lentils would be carefully placed in a brown bag. It was an important side dish for us and it was their way of saying they loved us and cared for us and wanted us to have good, nourishing food.

Let's Put Lentils In McDonald's

Wouldn't it be a wonderful idea if McDonald's sold lentils. And, instead of eating it there, they would provide take-out portions . . . so the entire family could enjoy the robust, energizing benefits of lentils . . . right in their own home . . . quietly, peacefully without the hustle of fast-food fare restaurants. Who knows . . . with such peaceful surroundings, you may get to know your wife again . . . and your children. And in like proportion as you eat lentils . . . the problems of the day will fade away.

Take Away French Fries

I would like to believe that! And I do!

It's time we get lentils back into the health food and medical textbooks. If you have to take out something to make space for it. Take out french fries! But never, never whisper a disparaging remark about lentils! Remember what happened to General Marcus Licinius Crassus!

AUNT WADIA'S LENTIL PARADISE   8 Servings
(SEE PHOTOGRAPH IN COLOR SECTION)

Aunt Wadia (Wah-dee-ah) was my favorite aunt. She helped my mother raise Lafayette, my sister Elsie and me. She did much of the cooking at our home. We were poor and this dish, called in Lebanese "mujadarra," (also called Imjadara) is considered a dish of the poor. It is an excellent protein dish. In the Middle East it is eaten as you and I would eat a breakfast cereal in the morning. This dish can be eaten either cold or hot! It sticks to your ribs and is high in mineral nourishment! I would choose **MUJADARRA** any day over food of the kings! Lentils are very, very inexpensive as well. It is far better to serve a lentil dish than meat ... and you save money, too! You may wish to presoak lentils overnight to cut down on cooking time. Take:

2 cups brown lentils

and cover with water. Get water boiling, then allow to simmer from 3/4 to 1½ hours or until tender.

While you are watching this paradise of power, take a frying pan and add:

4 tablespoons olive oil
2 onions finely chopped

Heat until soft and golden in hue. Add this to the lentils at the end of the simmering cycle when the lentils are done. Season with your favorite herb seasonings. Now, add:

½ cup long-grain rice, washed*

Add more water if needed, perhaps 2 cups of water. Simmer again for about 20 minutes, adding a little more water if it becomes absorbed too quickly. This is important: This combination should not be soupy but it should be fluid ... not dry looking. Enough liquid is needed to make it fluid but not so much that it becomes a soup. You may wish to drain a little liquid off at the end of simmering period. After a couple of tries you will come up with the combination you like best. Now for the topping, take:

2 onions sliced into half moon slivers
2-3 tablespoons olive oil

Place these slivers in the very hot olive oil in the frying pan and fry until dark brown and almost crisp. Serve the lentils on a regular dinner plate topping them off with the sprinkling of fried, half-moon slivers of onions. Mmmnn! I wish I had some right now!

* You may wish to use only ¼ cup rice. You can also substitute wild rice.

LAFAYETTE'S LENTIL SOUP   6 Servings

Why Lafayette? Well, that's my brother's name and I thought he would like a soup named after him. Best to presoak the lentils overnight. In the morning, rub them together in the water, removing their outer skin. Some prefer with skin, others without. Try it both ways.

In a large saucepan, melt:

4 tablespoons butter

and toss in:

1 large onion chopped
1 stalk celery with leaves, chopped
1 carrot chopped

for a brief moment to soften. Then with a joy beyond description, add:

7½ cups water*
1½ cups lentils
1 marrow bone cracked

Bring this to a boil. Skim off the gook that rises to the top. Simmer this combination for at least 3/4 of an hour and up to 1½ hours . . . until the lentils are soft. (If pre-soaked, simmering time is shortened) I don't like the lentils mushy but rather soft, yet firm. When the lentils are cooked, add:

Juice of 1 lemon
1 teaspoon ground cumin

Simmer a few minutes more and then remove the marrow bone. Now comes the touch of Lafayette: Take:

3 garlic cloves crushed
A pinch of cayenne pepper

and place in 3 tablespoons olive oil and stir thoroughly. Then add to soup and simmer for just 2 more minutes. (For a lighter soup, add a little more water when simmering)

* It is best to use 7½ cups meat stock if possible. This will give a richer, robust flavor.

If you forgot to presoak your lentils, the sky will not fall down. It simple means you may have to simmer the soup for 1½ hours instead of 3/4 of an hour.

AUNT EFFIE . . .
Why is Bertha always tired?

I have never seen her in a pair of pants that had much slack in them! Honestly. Some women grow old gracefully — others wear stretch pants. Bertha looks as though she had been poured into her clothes and had forgotten to say "when."

Bertha better learn to shuffle off the soufflés and park the pies! I don't know why she spends so much time at a hamburger joint. Those hamburgers and french fries will throw a monkey wrench in her engine and that bun will clog her colon! The Coke will give her a temporary lift then drop her quicker than a cow can flick off a fly!

With everything so high these days you would think Bertha would stay off those TV dinners and desserts. She works day and night to pay off that car. Why with gas prices so high, when I pulled into a station this morning and asked for a dollar's worth of gas . . . the attendant dabbed some behind my ears.

Bertha's tired because she eats "tired foods."

Bertha can't exist on Cheerios, Big Macs and chocolate chip cookies. She needs foods that provide vitality and energy without adding fat. It's about time she got acquainted with lentils. Lentils are a stick-to-your-ribs protein food . . . 25% protein and high in potassium, which is an excellent heart regulator and waste disposer.

12

OKRA . . . The Unknown Soldier of Vegetables

Okra? What in the world is an Okra?

Don't laugh!

But Christopher Columbus did not set out on his dangerous journey to America in search of fabled riches. Actually, Queen Isabella sent him to bring back the Okra!

Well, that really is not true! But so little is written about the Okra that I had to invent something!

Capitalize
The
Lowly Okra

The Okra,
and I capitalize the Okra everywhere
it appears
because it gets so little recognition
that I, personally have raised it to a status
of a Capitalized Word!

Anyway, the Okra is a tall annual plant. Okra is a kind of hibiscus. The hibiscus is noted for its large, colorful flowers.

The Okra is also closely related to cotton. Back in 1216 A.D., a Spaniard found it growing along the Nile River in Egypt. It reached Brazil by 1686. It is a native of Africa and quite naturally made its way to the southern part of the United States, where it is raised in large quantities for use in soups and stews. They know it as <u>gumbo or okro</u>. Most northerners and westerners would not know Okra. Some would think it was a disease!

Forgetting a Faithful Friend

Actually, here I sit at my typewriter absolutely frustrated! I have searched through all the major food books that claim to publish all there is to know about food and its history and many even do not include Okra! What a way to treat an old friend! A friend who has faithfully served through the centuries.

Why I dare say, even you have eaten Okra and never knew it! Remember eating that delicious soup with those green pinwheels floating all around. That, my friend, was Okra.

Why is Okra the Unknown Soldier of Vegetables?

It is bad enough that Okra puts its life on the line for soups and stews. But what adds insult to injury is that even in spite of this great sacrifice, no one knows who or what or why Okra is!

National Okra Day

Has anyone ever erected a statue to the Okra? Why hasn't the President of the United States declared July 5th as National Okra Day. After all, if we can celebrate July 4th as Independence Day, why can't we celebrate July 5th as independence from dull eating and the discovering of the Okra!

No one has even written an Ode to the Okra. We all can remember Joyce Kilmer's, <u>Tree</u>, but what about Okra? In fact, right now, let me be the first to write an Ode to the Okra. <u>It is</u>

Aunt Effie asks the question:

IF HISTORY COULD BE RE-WRITTEN
And the Presidents had recognized **OKRA** . . .
Would there be Peace?

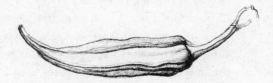

Mr. Kissinger and I have reviewed the matter with the Security Council. We feel that the institution of a National Okra Day would have changed the course of history. And, I might add, would have assured me of another term as President!

Based on the sound recommendations of my brother, Billy and Walter Cronkite, I am sending a bill to Congress for a National Okra Day. I believe it is time we recognize the human rights of vegetables. For too long Okra has served silently in the shadow behind peas and carrots (and peanuts).

**An
Historic
First**

<u>a first</u>. You are seeing it first here. Later on you may see this poem emblazoned on page 1 of The New York Times, and memorialized in bronze in the White House portico.

ODE TO THE OKRA

I think that I shall never see
The Okra reach its destiny
This precious pod of rib-bed spine
Should make the front cover of TIME

Of all the wars in which it's fought
In soups and stews and motley lot
Its victories no one could see
It's destined for ambiguity.

But I for one will not sit still
While Okra takes the bitter pill
It's time to stick close to this friend
And fight until the very end.

Okra, oh, dear Okra, I shall ne'er forget
The many, warm days in which we met

As you kissed my lips and warmed me through
And snuggled in my tummy, too.

America, awake! Shun the cakes and pies
The hamburgers, the Cokes and the french fries
<u>Remember the OKRA!</u> is our victory cry!
Let's make it as American as apple pie!

In appreciation, by Salem Kirban

Out of difficulties grow miracles. And I believe the Okra is a miracle plant, good for most everyone. Okra grows from 2 to 8 feet. The pods on the plant (and that is what you eat) are from 4 to 6 inches, and they can exceed a foot. However, they are best picked when they are young and tender at 3 to 4 inches. They literally grow an inch or two overnight once they start maturing.

A Most Wonderful Memory

As a child I can remember my mother preparing a most delicious Lebanese dish featuring Okra. She called it bamia (bā-mee) which is Arabic. The English call it "ladies' fingers." She used this Okra in a lamb stew along with tomatoes and onions and sometimes stringbeans.

Within the Okra pod are little pods surrounded by a glutinous or sticky substance which holds the whole thing together. And in a stew, this permeates the contents and imparts its delicate flavor throughout.

Rich in Minerals

Okra is rich in Vitamins A and B, plus iron and phosphorus. Symptoms of a lack of phosphorus in the body may include: neuralgia, impotence, numbness in some part of the body, bronchitis and beanlike knots forming in glands in the neck.

There are large and dwarf varieties of Okra. The dwarf variety is the more popular because their pods ripen earlier. The ripe seeds in Okra have even been used as a substitute for coffee!

To me, Okra is an oasis in the supermarket wasteland. You will find this friend in the frozen section, in the canned section but seldom will you find it in the fresh vegetable section. In fact, seldom will you find it . . . period. Okra is the unknown soldier of vegetables. And it's time we pay respect to this faithful friend.

Mary Kirban, author's wife, relaxes by the garden with one of our famous tomato sandwiches. The tomato was just picked right off the vine pictured in the background of photo. It is sliced into thick 3/4″ slices, sprinkled liberally with garlic and cayenne pepper and topped with freshly picked mint. The roses are from our front yard.

Darrell Kirban and his grandfather put together circular tomato supports in early June. Grandfather? Am I really that old? Well, working in the garden and eating its nutritious harvest makes me feel young again!

In August, 1976, our daughter, Doreen and her husband, Wes, moved from Pennsylvania to the state of Washington with their two children, Jessica and Joshua. They lived on the side of a mountain in a log-type cabin with no modern facilities.

Mother and daughter embrace in a laughing and tearful reunion.

Their faces reflect the joy of reunion. For complete story, see page 41.

A handful of cherry tomatoes represent just a small portion of the abundance of crop that grew in our backyard garden. Note eggplant resting on author's foot, ready for picking.

Here is an excellent food value ... LENTILS! I call it Aunt Wadia's
Lentil Paradise. You will find the receipe on page 138. We included the
package in this photograph because most people are not familiar with
lentils. They generally are found in the dried bean section of your
supermarket. Lentils are very high in potassium and an excellent protein dish ... even for breakfast. You can make lentils come alive by
adding onion and tomato slices and of course, parsley!

Doreen Frick, author's daughter, cultivates the hot pepper patch. On the recommendation of Dr. Reams we grew our peppers 25 feet away from our regular garden. Doreen does necessary cultivating in mid-June.

Above is just a small indication of the beautiful harvest we have in hot peppers. We had so many that we put quite a few in the freezer and enjoyed them all the way into the next spring! They are really delicious!

Author preparing soil prior to planting carrots. Carrots need soil that is loose and aerated for a depth of 12 inches. Peat moss in channel is mixed with earth to make a loose loam. Such preparation makes a rich harvest. Photo taken in early June shows the first of four stages of garden growth.

Mary Kirban views garden in late June to check progress. To the right are onions (some planted the year before), lettuce, broccoli, carrots, zucchini squash and tomato plants. Note their growth in the photos on the next page. Also observe the marigolds we planted completely around garden.

Photo taken in July reflects growth that comes with tender loving care and applying the right nutrients to the soil. Mary Kirban stands by circular tomato supports. Bird feeder is in foreground.

Last photograph taken in August shows Duane Kirban marveling at growth in our backyard garden. The tomato plants were loaded with tomatoes. Note the row of Okra at right of photograph and the flourishing marigolds.

At the back of our house is our comfrey plant. It grows without much care. My wife, Mary, holds the beautiful comfrey blossoms in her hand.

Here I am gathering parsley from my parsley bed to make that salad of all salads I call Salem's Salad. It is really the Lebanese <u>Tabbouleh</u>.

The stately and proud Okra plant. We plant an entire row of these every year. Note the beautiful blossom! The Okra pods are almost ready for harvest.

For a hearty and nutritious meal try something different . . . try Chicken and Okra Soup. You will find the recipe of page 146.

Garlic, onions and peppers . . . the Big Three of the flavor family, get together for a grand reunion! Isn't time you became friends with this nutritious trio? Such a reunion will bring tears of joy to your eyes!

It was a hot June day and I had spent most of that Saturday weeding and cultivating. I deserved a watermelon break at 3 PM. Incidentally, watermelon is best eaten alone and not with a meal. Learn to take a break and relax!

(Photo by Diane Kirban, Prairie Bible Institute campus)

Would you like to enjoy a refreshing rainbow of good health? If you have been through a storm of illness, you can appreciate the hope for better health. For how to regain or maintain a rainbow of good health, see the next page.

A STAGNANT POOL **A GENTLE, FLOWING STREAM**

Take a mental photograph of your meal each time you sit down to eat. Ask yourself the question: *"Is the food I am about to eat going to help make my body a stagnant pool or will this food make my body a gentle, flowing stream?"* If you do this honestly, chances are your eating habits will change and your overall health will improve.

**Remember
The
Okra!**

Now you may not fall head over heels in love with Okra as a long-lost friend. But do not use a hatchet to remove a fly from your friend's forehead. When you take your children to the supermarket with you, or even your husband, as you approach the area where Okra resides, caution your family to speak in hushed, reverent tones and with deep respect.

And next July 5th, hang out the flag and celebrate National OKRA Day over a cup of coffee.

Who knows? The coffee you are drinking may be made from crushed Okra seeds. Now what other friend would make such a sacrifice as to contribute his life's blood on the hallowed grounds of coffee?

Remember the OKRA! is our victory cry! Let's make it as American as apple pie!-

I thank you.
My friends thank you.
And Okra thanks you!

President Nixon, accompanied by Anwar Sadat, waves to enthusiastic crowds who have just been told that the President had recorded the National Okra Day theme song in Arabic. (Later developments show that it was accidentally erased in a 5-minute gap on the tape recorder)

CHICKEN & OKRA SOUP
6 Servings

(SEE PHOTOGRAPH IN COLOR SECTION)

Get ready for a real, hearty, taste treat on a cold winter's evening or a bright, summer's day. (And, if you are reading this in the winter, plan now to plant Okra this spring. It's easy to grow and has beautiful flowers) OK! First secure:

6 cups chicken broth

Place chicken broth in large kettle or Dutch oven. And then combine chicken broth with:

1 can (1 pound) whole tomatoes
1 onion diced (about ½ cup)
1 package (10 ounces) frozen whole or cut Okra*
1 can (7 ounces) whole kernel corn
½ cup uncooked long grain rice
2 teaspoons sea salt or herb seasoning
½ teaspoon paprika
½ teaspoon liquid hot pepper seasoning

Now bring this glorious masterpiece to a boil, stirring often. (With that hot pepper in there; sniff the fumes emanating from the pot and it will clear your sinus in a hurry) Once pot boils, lower heat; cover and simmer 40 minutes.
Now, add:

3 cups cooked chicken, diced

Stir and heat this combination through, adding additional seasoning if desired.

There it is . . . in all its glory! Now, if you wish to thicken broth a little . . . after you take Chicken and Okra Soup off stove; add 1 or 2 teaspoons tapioca flour.

* It's really a sin to cut Okra. All the good "gook" runs out! If you grow Okra in your backyard farm, cut off pod when it is about 2" to 2½" long and put the whole pod in your soup.

OKRA ARABIC
4-6 Servings

Here is a popular dish that can be served hot or cold. Close your eyes and pretend you are lost on a hot desert. Sand is swirling all around you. Suddenly the wind stops and on the horizon you see a dashing Arab prince riding towards you on a camel with a dish of Okra Arabic. Your eyes light up. Okra again has come to the rescue!

Now, in a large saucepan, heat:

7 tablespoons olive oil

And place in saucepan and fry:

¾ lb. white button onions
3 cloves garlic, halved

until this combination is slightly soft and transparent. Then add:

2 lbs. fresh young Okra (or 28-oz. can Okra with liquid)*

and continue to fry until slightly softened. Now, add:

1 lb. tomatoes, peeled and sliced

and sauté for a few minutes longer. Season to taste with herb seasonings. Cover this combination with water, bring to a boil, and simmer until the Okra is very tender. This will probably take about 1 hour. And what would Okra be without lemon! So, now squeeze:

Juice of 1 lemon

and cook 15 minutes longer.

For added flavor you may wish to add:

1 teaspoon ground coriander
2 cloves crushed garlic

This dish can be served hot or cold.
* If canned Okra is used, a shorter cooking time is required.

AUNT EFFIE . . .
There's a splinter in my cottage cheese!

What do you expect for 55¢ . . . the whole cottage! If more people in the world ate Okra they wouldn't be so mentally confused. The way these politicians are running the country the cost of living is going up and the chance of living is going down. Inflation hasn't ruined everything. A dime can still be used as a screwdriver. Americans are getting stronger. Twenty years ago it took two people to carry $10 worth of groceries. Today, a five-year-old does it! I've never seen so many confused people as I see today. They follow the leader. They can't think for themselves. And those doctors stuff them with Valium to give them further memory loss. Okra is a quick memory pepper-upper!

Tell them to eat Okra and it's like telling them to bathe in the river Jordan! Okra is high in calcium. That gives vitality and endurance and reduces tension. Anyone who is tense depletes their calcium quickly. And potassium? Wow! Is Okra loaded with potassium. Potassium is the electricity for the heart . . . keeps it in rhythm. A lack of potassium can cause weak muscles, constipation, and nervous tension.

Never cut the ends of the Okra pods! That way, the gelatin won't run out and you'll get the full benefit. Best way to cook it is to steam it. Delicious with lemon juice!

13

GARLIC, THE POOR MAN'S RICHES

If I had to choose between gold and garlic, I'd choose GARLIC . . . for it is nature's gold.

Sophisticated people tend to shy away from it . . . for it has a pungent aroma that broadcasts without a radio!

Pets apparently love it and thrive on it . . . for most brands of pet food contain garlic.

Actually garlic comes from a well-bred line. It is part of the lily family, a cousin. But there is always one black sheep in the family.

Garlic A Medicine Used By Egyptians
For thousands of years garlic has been accepted as both a food and a medicine. The Egyptians had at least 22 therapeutic formulas using garlic about 2000 B.C. It was used for headaches, heart problems, body weakness, worms, problems of childbirth. The Egyptians even used it in their enemas! To them garlic was a god!

The Israelites had a hard time in Egypt. They were slaves and most were assigned to brickmaking. Pharoah made the task of brickmaking as difficult as possible. He did not supply the necessary straw for the bricks.

The Israelites had to go search for it wherever they could find it. Hebrew officers were assigned to make sure the job got done. When quotas were not fulfilled, it was the Hebrew overseer who suffered.

From Suffering

He was made to lie on his stomach with his legs and feet upward. He would be struck many blows on the soles of his feet. This made it impossible for him to walk for weeks.

The Israelites began to murmur against Moses and Aaron, blaming them for Pharoah's oppressive attitude.

When Moses finally did lead the some 6 million Israelites out of Egypt, thru the Red Sea and into the wilderness, the people still were not satisfied.

To Murmuring

All along the way they were complaining. Somehow they seemed to forget the unbearable demands of Pharoah and longed for the peasant food that they had once relished. And they complained to Moses:

> We remember the fish, which we did eat in Egypt freely; the cucumbers and the melons, and the leeks, and the onions and the garlic.
>
> (Numbers 11:5)

Moses was at the end of his rope. He had had it with the complaints of the Israelites and in Numbers 11:15 went so far as to ask God to kill him and release him from this continual round of complaints heaped upon him by his people. Even Moses was human and the pressure was getting to him. In those days there was no Vitamin B complex capsules and Vi-

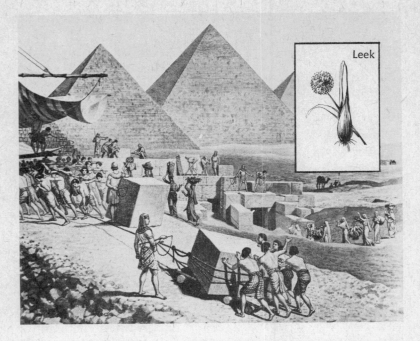

Leek

Garlic is only mentioned once in the Bible. After Moses had successfully guided the Israelites to safety from Pharaoh, they still yearned for the "... leeks and the onions and the garlic" of Egypt (Numbers 11:5). Their memories were short. They apparently forgot about the oppression of slavery that was their lot under Pharaoh.

Charcoal roasted whole garlic is still a Middle Eastern specialty. Place whole bulbs of garlic directly on the coals of a grille (but not in flaming fire). The cloves are ready when they are browned and tender. If you wish, you can marinate beforehand. You can baste the garlic heads with oil and herb seasonings after you remove from fire. The meat can be easily pushed out of the hardened skin. An excellent nutlike flavor. Garlic is rich in phosphorus and potassium. It has a high sulphur content. Sulphur has been termed the "beauty mineral" and is vital for healthy hair, skin and nails.

The leek (pictured in inset) resembles an onion. Leeks are very high in potassium and are excellent to use in soups.

tamin C chewables to relieve his stress.
But he could have eaten the garlic!

Wherever the Israelites had a garden, you could count on it containing garlic, onions and leeks.

**Garlic
A
Marital Aid**

The people of Israel believed that garlic, considered a "hot" food, had generative powers that gave the body life and marital energy.

The Talmud suggested the eating of garlic for gynecological and menstrual disturbances. Even in Russia and Poland today, Jews break their fast on bread and raw garlic.

Garlic, in fact, has a long history . . . going back much further than the times of Egyptian oppression of the people of Israel. The Chinese have used garlic for centuries.

**A
Healing
Food**

In fact, one peculiar fact about garlic should be noted. Almost always it is the food of the poor people. Garlic was even used by the Babylonians about 3000 B.C.! All believed in the healing powers of garlic.

The Greeks loved garlic. In fact the famous Greek philosopher Aristotle (384 B.C.) said of garlic:

> It is a cure for hydrophobia and as tonic, is hot, laxative . . .

Hippocrates (460 B.C.) praised garlic as a medicine that promotes perspiration and both as a laxative and diuretic (medicine to aid in the secretion of urine).

Garlic was used in the Olympic Games by the athletes to increase their stamina.

The respected Roman physician, Galen (A.D.

131-200) spoke highly of garlic. Modern medicine considers Galen the father of medicine, incidentally. Galen believed that garlic helped to eradicate toxins from the bloodstream.

**The
Dark Age
Of Medicine**

It is only that as we became more "knowledgeable" that we substituted antibiotics. Harry G. Bieler, M.D., in his book, <u>Food Is Your Best Medicine</u>, says:

> *Today we are in the ... Antibiotic Age. Unhappily, too, this is the Dark Age of Medicine — an age in which many of my colleagues, when confronted with a patient, consult a volume which rivals the Manhattan telephone directory in size. This book contains the names of thousands upon thousands of drugs used to alleviate the distressing symptoms of a host of diseased states of the body. The doctor then decides which pink or purple or baby-blue pill to prescribe for the patient.*[1]

As we near the close of the Twentieth Century, perhaps more doctors will see the value of old-fashioned remedies like garlic.

The Chinese used garlic to preserve fresh meat. In fact it has been found to have an antimicrobial effect on meat.

Cortez, conqueror of Mexico, discovered that the natives *"esteem garlic above all the roots of Europe."*

For centuries the people of Bulgaria have made garlic a part of their daily diet! They

---

[1] Henry G. Bieler, M.D., <u>Food is Your Best Medicine</u> (New York: Random House), 1965, p. 13.

chew garlic just as some people would chew tobacco. And Bulgarians are noted for their long life! Many of them still work a full day at 100 years of age. Could this remarkable herb, garlic, play an important part in the longevity of this very robust race of people?

Provides Stamina and Strength

Garlic is still a mainstay in the Middle East. This tradition goes back to Egyptian days when Pharaoh made sure the Israelities had plenty of garlic to eat. In the building of the pyramids, garlic was one of the main vegetables supplied in large quantities to the workers. In fact one of the first sit-down strikes to occur in history occurred during the building of the pyramid Cheops. They stopped working because their daily supply of garlic had been withheld! They knew they needed this herb for stamina, strength and endurance. If 5000 years ago common laborers knew the value of garlic, how much more enlightened should we be to its attributes now in the 20th Century!

Even today building and engineering experts are baffled as to how human energy was able to construct these colossal pyramids. Maybe if we ate garlic every day, we, too, could perform wonders!

The Mystery of Marseilles

In 1721, the bustling seaport of Marseilles, France, suffered a terrible plague. Thousands upon thousands of people were dying like flies. The officials found it extremely difficult to find anyone who would bury them. They finally released four convicts who had previously been sentenced to death. It was their job to bury the dead.

Four Thieves Vinegar

Something unusual happened. The convicts appeared to be immune from the terrible plague. They were offered their freedom if they would divulge the secret of what kept them from the dread disease. They admitted that each day they drank wine loaded with garlic. This drink is still famous today. It is called "Four Thieves Vinegar."

Benjamin Franklin discovered that the farm people of France always included a diet of garlic for 3 weeks upon the onset of Spring. And doctors carried cloves of garlic to safeguard themselves from disease.

Of all the countries in past history, Great Britain possessed a people who disdained garlic. Perhaps that is why during plagues, the English paid a bitter price for neglecting this apple of nature's gold.

As Valuable As Money

To the Siberians garlic was as valuable as money. They paid their taxes in garlic; 5 bulbs for a child, 10 bulbs for a woman and 15 bulbs for a man. That gives me an idea. I think I'll pay my income tax in garlic bulbs. The nation may be healthier for it!

Russian Penicillin

The Chinese and the Russians do not shy away from old-fashioned remedies for illness. In fact, Soviet scientists use what is termed "Russian Penicillin." It is a distillation of garlic (Allicin) which kills only unhealthy bacteria and leave the natural healthy bacteria alone, reports Lloyd J. Harris, in his excellent book, The Book of Garlic.

Doctors used garlic extensively during the 18th and 19th centuries. However, since

World War 2, we have changed over from natural healing herbal remedies to drugs. Prior to World War 2, patients were not bombarded with an avalanche of drugs. Herbal medicines were respected. They had no side effects and patients did not become addicts. They received treatment as God provided it, right from the earth!

A Common Remedy

It may be hard for some to realize that every plant is a miracle. And many doctors are now coming to realize garlic's medicinal power. Garlic is a strong antiseptic, a germicidal agent and has disease-preventitive qualities. For centuries, garlic has been a common remedy for colds in many European countries.

Studies in the University of Geneva have indicated that blood pressure was effectively lowered in many patients who had high blood pressure and included garlic in their diet. Garlic appears to open blood vessels, thus reducing the blood pressure. In these same studies patients noted that dizziness, angina and headaches often disappeared!

Garlic's Secret Ingredient

Garlic is an antiseptic. It is credited with saving thousands of lives in World War 1.

While garlic is rich in vitamins and minerals, its secret powers lie in only 2% content of the product — that which makes it smell. It is called allyd disulphate. This potent, essential, natural oil is the power behind the throne! It is nature's penicillin!

What medicinal properties are attributed to garlic!

First, it is a supreme antiseptic. A majority of people suffer from bad eating habits. Toxins build up in their system. They complain of colds, allergies, headaches. Garlic has been found as a purifier . . . nature's purifier, a powerful antiseptic! In his book, About Garlic, G. J. Binding writes:

Nature's Purifier

> Garlic should not only be used when one becomes ill, for in vegetable, tablet or capsule form it can work miracles in keeping the system free from poisons. Best used as a preventive treatment supplementary to the diet.[1]

I personally have found this to be true, taking 4 (15-grain) tablets at each meal.

---

[1] G. J. Binding, F.R.H.S., About Garlic, the Supreme Herbal Remedy (Wellingborough, England: Thorsons Publishers, Ltd), 1970, p. 52.

Athletes in the Greek Olympics used garlic for endurance and stamina. Perhaps the runner pictured above could have used a couple cloves of garlic before the race!

Not only is garlic considered a supreme antiseptic but also an efficient cleanser of the blood and tissues. Some have found it excellent for alleviating diarrhea. Others use it for fevers. Many have used it for the pains associated with rheumatism and arthritis.

For Aches and Pains

Some in the medical establishment would look at garlic as an excellent food flavorer but downgrade its healing properties.

However, if it was good enough for the Israelites, it's good enough for me. And that's going some . . . considering my parents are of Arab heritage! But Arab and Jew alike have discovered the remarkable properties of garlic. Unfortunately the garlic one buys in stores in the United States is rather anemic compared to the large, bulbous garlic available in the Middle East. I can remember how shocked I was to see donkeys loaded down with garlic bulbs in Jerusalem . . . shocked because the garlic bulbs were as big as oranges!

For High Blood Pressure

Over the years garlic has been used in the treatment of cholera and typhus by Dr. Albert Schweitzer. Garlic has been used by those suffering from asthma and tuberculosis, high blood pressure (hypertension) and even cancer!

Many people think that garlic is indigestible. They will be surprised to learn that, on the contrary, garlic greatly aids digestion and promotes the health of the stomach. It is an extremely valuable food. You recall my mentioning that athletes in the Greek Olympics used garlic for endurance and stamina.

For Failing Memory

Mrs. Eleanor Roosevelt, at a late age, was asked what was the secret of her remarkable memory.

She replied: "Garlic cloves!"

She had read that garlic was an old, folk remedy for failing memory. So she faithfully consumed three honey-covered cloves every morning.

For Asthma

Farmers in England use garlic as a remedy for asthma. Others rub pimples and other skin irritations with garlic several times a day. They claim this makes the skin problem disappear without leaving any scars! Garlic is considered a sedative for the stomach. Most people prefer to take garlic in capsule form because of its strong flavor.

I can still picture my mother using garlic in making that famous Lebanese salad called Tabbouleh (pronounced tah-boo-lee).[1] We lived on a little farm in Schultzville, Pennsylvania near Clarks Summit and Scranton. It was the depression days of the early 1930's. Garlic to us was gold . . . more precious than gold! The preparation of this salad was almost a ritual.

My mother would get a large garlic bulb, peel the cloves, then slice the cloves real thin. These slices would be put into a large cup with just a covering of pure olive oil. For several minutes she would painstakingly crush the slices of garlic until the aroma had penetrated the olive oil.

When this was done, she would add more

---

[1] The recipe for Tabbouleh can be found in **HOW TO EAT YOUR WAY BACK TO VIBRANT HEALTH** by Salem Kirban. $3.95.

olive oil, filling the cup. The essence of garlic-oil would then be stirred to permeate the entire contents. The ritual was completed. Prior to this she had prepared all the other ingredients for the Tabbouleh salad.

**Liquid
Gold**

Carefully she poured this liquid gold over the salad. And then the secret! She left the salad "rest" for one day in our ice box. Overnight the garlic was celebrating a marriage as it wedded itself to the parsley, the scallions, the mint, the bulgur wheat and the tomatoes. What a wedding!

The next day . . . what a feast! It was a food too good for the selective palates of Presidents and Kings and Queens. It was a food for we peasants, who didn't have two dimes to rub together, for we knew the secret of God's garlic. Yes, if I had to choose between gold and garlic, I would choose GARLIC . . . for it is nature's GOLD!

GARLIC AND HAS/BEAN VEGETABLE SOUP   10 Servings

What? You never heard of a Has/Bean Soup? Well, this soup <u>has beans</u> in it! This soup is loaded with amino acids. It gives you complete protein without eating bread! First, the night before, plan to presoak:

½ cup dried beans
½ cup wild rice

(Tell them it's their Saturday night bath as you draw the bath water) On the day you are making your soup, cook the beans and rice and save the water these are cooked in for use later on in recipe.

The first thing you do is stir-fry in your large soup pot:

5 onions chopped (medium
onions)
2 green peppers chopped
4 cloves garlic, mashed
Sufficient olive oil to stir fry
above

Then with hilarity, add:

1 teaspoon dried basil
2 teaspoons dried parsley
1 teaspoon dried oregano

and continue to stir-fry for two minutes. Then, with joy in your heart, stir in:

7 large fresh tomatoes chopped
(or 1 quart canned tomatoes)

To this add:

1 bay leaf
A tinch of cayenne pepper[1]

Cover the pot and allow this mixture to simmer for a few minutes. You may add a little more water if it thickens too much. Then use your creative ability by adding:

3 carrots diced
1 turnip diced
1 parsnip diced
2 beets diced

And simmer for about 30 more minutes. Then add:

½ cup corn
1 cup green beans diced
1 cup Okra sliced

and simmer about 20 more minutes. Then add the wild rice and dried beans including the water that you cooked them in. Also add:

½ cup cabbage
½ cup kale
½ cup peas

Cook a few more minutes. Just before eating, top the soup with fresh parsley and scallions or chives.

1 *Tinche: In our household, whenever we indicate just a pinch of something, we say "tinche." Just a little bit of bright information I thought I would add to lighten your day.*

(Basic suggestions: Courtesy PRE-VENTION Magazine)

GARLIC SOUP
8 Servings

Who ever heard of garlic soup? One might think this would have a very strong garlic flavor . . . but it is surprisingly mild. It is a refreshing winter soup and so beneficial for you. And garlic is so cheap!

With a joy and zest for living, go down to your supermarket and quickly grab:

2 large heads fresh garlic

Tenderly separate the heads of garlic into cloves. Place the cloves in a cup and while they are not looking, pour boiling water all over them! Then undress them by slipping off their skins. Now drop them in a kettle with:

- **2 quarts water**
- **2 tablespoons sea salt**
- **¼ teaspoon cayenne pepper**
- **2 whole cloves**
- **¼ teaspoon sage**
- **¼ teaspoon thyme**
- **5 sprigs parsley**
- **2 tablespoons oil**

Bring to a boil and then let simmer for 30 minutes.

Awaken the chicken and take from her:

- **3 eggs**
- **¼ cup melted butter**

Beat these together vigorously so they get fully acquainted and become fast friends. Meanwhile, back at the ranch, take that simmering pot with all the water in it and strain the soup mixture. To the strained liquid, slowly add the egg mixture beating the liquid with vigor as you add. Reheat but do not boil. Your soup is now ready to partake.

If you want to live dangerously, don't bother straining the soup. Sip up the dregs and all!

AUNT EFFIE . . .
Poor Alphonso has arteriosclerosis!

That's just a big name for hardening of the arteries! Several things happen and it just doesn't occur overnight. Your blood vessels are like the new pipes you installed in your house. You start running some adulterated water through and over the years lime deposits build up and the inside diameter of the pipe narrows. Same with Alphonso's blood vessels. Wrong eating habits, slowly over the years, have made his arteries become thick with gunk. The passage way for the blood becomes narrower, the walls of the blood vessels lose their elasticity. Soon he becomes forgetful. Blood pressure increases. He gets cramps in his legs and notices circulation problems.

Atherosclerosis is a form of arteriosclerosis and both are no bonanza! They cause most of the heart attacks and strokes. So Alphonso better "fasta from the pasta." Did you know he wears a girdle? A girdle is a device to keep an unfortunate situation from spreading!

Granny Osgood has a good remedy for high blood pressure and artery problems. She drinks 4 ounces of carrot juice mixed with 3 ounces of pineapple juice. She drinks this and eats three honey-covered garlic cloves every morning. Alphonso may want to substitute garlic perles he can buy at the health food store.

14

PARSLEY . . . The Forgotten Food

Parsley is like the second verse of a hymn . . .
It is there . . . but seldom used!

What? You ask . . . is parsley really a food?
Why I thought it was a garnish.

How in the world can you exile parsley to
such an inauspicious role!

A garnish is just a decoration . . . an adorn-
ment . . . an embellishment!

**The
Misuse of
Parsley**

Caterers painstakingly place parsley on their
main dishes they serve in banquets throughout the world. And a recent news report indicates that same parsley comes right back to
them and they throw thousands of tons of it
away in the garbage cans.

What a pity!

You go to a restaurant to eat. And what do
they serve you? Bacon and fried eggs plus
they throw a little green stuff on the plate to
give the plate color. After all, all good cooks
know, that regardless how bad the food, if the
platter is colorful . . . you will eat it and think
it was a good meal.

And you do. That is, you do eat the bacon (which is not good for you) and the fried egg (which is equally as bad). And that green stuff . . . the poor lonely parsley . . . who never hurt anyone in his life, never stepped on a spider or took a lollipop away from a baby. What do you do with the parsley? NOTHING! ABSO-LUTELY NOTHING. You leave it on your plate and destine it to the garbage heap.

And you wonder why you get sick!

Change Your Eating Habits

The next time you have bacon and eggs, push the bacon and eggs away for the garbage heap and eat the green parsley. And you'll be far healthier for it. And, if you are out with friends, gather up all their parsley (for most restaurants are miserly with their parsley) and promptly proceed to eat it. Have you ever eaten a parsley sandwich? Tremendous with a slice of tomato!

Now your friends will think you're a bit strange! HO! HO! Look at John. He's gone bananas . . . eating parsley. But you'll have the last laugh as you visit them in the hospital in later years!

Several months ago I went to a Marriott chain restaurant called The Hot Shoppes. They had a lovely cafeteria style food counter. Sur-rounding the cakes and pies and other food was huge bunches of bright, green parsley. My how my heart leaped. Quickly I grabbed for a handful only to be admonished by the waitress who said:

THAT'S FOR DECORATION!

And I didn't get far . . . because the parsley

was tightly tied in bunches and firmly secured to the counter!

Then in July, 1977 I attended the National Nutrition Foods Association convention in Las Vegas at the Hilton Hotel. Their cafeteria-style restaurant had a very ostentatious array of foods, much of it I would consider "dead" food. But surrounding all this was a fabulous display of rich, green parsley . . . the largest I had seen.

The Day I Grabbed The Parsley

By this time, I decided to put caution to the winds. I grabbed a fistful of parsley and it wouldn't budge. It was nailed down! To the amazement of those about me, including my associate, Bob Conner, I got out my trusty penknife and whacked off a handful of the parsley and put it on my plate. Quickly I by-passed the dead foods and the creamy pies and cakes. What a meal I had that day!

I say it is time for the Parsley Eaters of America to unite. We get concerned about oil spills in the ocean and oil getting on a duck's back (and rightly so)! Isn't it about time we

Next time don't give your sweetheart flowers. She can't eat them! Give her a bouquet of parsley and watch her face light up. Parsley is high in Vitamin A. It will make her skin lovelier and give her better vision to see the good points in you!

take a stand for dear old parsley. He doesn't belong in the garbage cans of America! He belongs in the stomachs of Americans (and all other people, too!).

**Richer
In
Vitamin C**

We have heard Anita Bryant sing the praises of orange juice (and particularly Florida orange juice). But why doesn't someone sing the praises of PARSLEY?

Actually, did you know that parsley has more Vitamin C than orange juice? Let's look at the comparison:

	Vitamin C content	
	8 ounces Orange Juice	**Full cup PARSLEY**
Fresh	130 mg.	140 mg.
Canned	99 mg.	
Frozen	112 mg.	

A glass of 8 ounces of orange juice averages 112 calories while a cup of parsley is only 20.

A glass of orange juice has only 500 mg. of Vitamin A. A cup of parsley has 6800 mg. of Vitamin A.

A glass of orange juice can give you an "energy drop." That's right, a let down!

Oranges just have such a large concentrate of sugar that many, upon drinking it, find that a few minutes later they have an energy DROP, fatigue sets in. Now, eating a whole orange (peeling it but including the white skin) will not give one this energy drop! This is particularly true with those people who suffer from low blood sugar (hypoglycemia).

If you don't feel like eating a whole orange, then why not switch to grapefruit juice. You won't get an energy drop! And while you're doing that, chomp on a couple sprigs of parsley.

A Miracle Plant

Parsley is one of nature's miracle plants! The Latin word for parsley is <u>petroselinum</u> (*petros*, a rock + *selinon*, celery). Actually parsley is a cousin to the carrot and celery as well as parsnip. There are at least 37 varieties of curly parsley alone. Although they are biennials (last for 2 years), they are best planted fresh each year in your garden or hotbed.

Parsley had a long and glorious life before sophisticated 20th Century diners started treating it as a second class citizen!

The Parsley Crown

It is said that none other than Hercules crowned himself with parsley. A similar crown was used as the prize for those winners in Greek games. Anacreon, the poet, upheld parsley as the emblem of joy and festivity. In the banqueting halls of Greece and Rome, parsley was worn as a head ornament.

In battle, the warriors of Homer fed their chariot horses with it.

Parsley appears to be of Egyptian origin and eventually worked its way to Europe and then to America.

One 19th century writer said that

if parsley is thrown into fish ponds
it will heal the sick fishes therein.

The Greeks also decorated their tombs with parsley. Greek legend has it that parsley sprang up where the blood of the Greek hero Archemorous had spilled when he was eaten by serpents. This brought about a common expression:

> if you are in need of parsley
> you must be seriously ill.

How much better to use parsley as a preventative than to suddenly show an interest in this forgotten herb when you become sick!

How To Grow Parsley

Anyone who has grown parsley has discovered it is slow to grow. Actually, it is best to soak the seeds overnight before planting to give the seeds a head start. Even at that it can take 60-80 days to mature. A superstition abounded that its slow growing was attributed to it having to go to Satan and back seven times. Others believed only a witch could grow it. Others believed a fine harvest could only be achieved if it were planted on Good Friday or by a pregnant woman.

An Excellent Diuretic

In Greek the word, parsley, means "stonebreaker." And even today, parsley is known as an excellent diuretic. Many consider it a beneficial herb to ease the pain of arthritis. In 164 A.D. Galen said parsley was "*sweet and grateful to the stomach.*"

Parsley was introduced into England about 1548 from Sardinia. It was largely used to make parsley pies!

What most people do not realize is that parsley is an excellent digestive aid. But, sad to say, the average individual will eat bacon and a fried egg for breakfast (both hard to digest) and then push aside the parsley which could aid them in their digestion.

Then for lunch, they will go to a restaurant and gulp down a hamburger and french fries (both loaded with fats) and again push aside the parsley.

The Parsley Cover Up

Parsley served on most platters is rather sickly and sparse. Perhaps it is recycled by the restaurant owner *"since no one eats the stuff anyway"*.

Parsley has long been recognized for its ability to overcome strong scents like garlic, as an example.

The most famous dish that incorporates parsley is the Lebanese or Middle East salad called Tabbouleh.[1] This is a bulgur (cracked wheat) salad which incorporates 1 cup of finely chopped parsley to serve 4-6 people. Also included in this salad are the bulgur, onions, ming, olive oil, lemon juice and garlic!

Eliminates Gas

Medicinally, parsley has been used for centuries to aid the stomach's digestive processes, to combat gas (flatulence), for gallstones and to insure sweet breath.

Those who would use parsley in a juice should be cautioned that parsley juice should never be taken in quantities of more than two ounces at a time and then it should be mixed with carrot or celery juice. The reason: The parsley juice is a high concentrate and large doses of juice concentrate can rapidly decrease blood pressure and cause other side effects.

No cautions are necessary when eating parsley in whole form with your meals or in a salad, like the Lebanese salad mentioned

---

[1] The recipe for Tabbouleh can be found in **HOW TO EAT YOUR WAY BACK TO VIBRANT HEALTH** by Salem Kirban. $3.95.

**The
Parsley-
Tomato
Sandwich**

previously. I often go out to the garden around lunchtime, take a ripe, juicy tomato off the vine, take 8 or 10 sprigs of fresh parsley from my garden. Bringing them in the house, I slice a one-inch slice of tomato, place it on a piece of bread . . . sprinkle the tomato with olive oil and garlic plus red cayenne pepper and top it off with parsley.

Wow! What a meal!

Ooops! It's 1:30 already. And you know what I'm going to do? You guessed it. I'm going to end this chapter right here . . . go out into my garden, pick a ripe, red tomato and make my-self the Kirban TOMATO-PARSLEY SANDWICH!

Why don't you join me?

Don't have any parsley?

Just walk in any restaurant, walk by 5 or 10 tables and quickly snatch the parsley off the customer's plates.

They will never miss it. But they may think you're crazy.

But honestly now, you and I are the only sane people left! So why don't we start a lobbying organization and call it I.P.P., the

International Organization
for the
Preservation and Promotion
of the
PARSLEY

And I'll tell you what. I'll step down and let you be President.

Meanwhile . . . back to my Kirban TOMATO-PARSLEY sandwich!

PARSNIP & PARSLEY SALAD
4 Servings

Never heard of a parsnip? Neither had I! Parsnips resemble carrots in shape. To bring out the best flavor in parsnips, store them for several weeks just a little above 32° in the frige. Parsnips discolor easily so do not peel them. Parsnips are rich in minerals.
Combine:

- **2 cups shredded, raw parsnips[1]**
- **1 cup fresh parsley finely cut[2]**
- **1 tomato chopped fine**
- **2 green onions chopped fine**
- **¼ cup quartered ripe olives**
- **1 cup celery finely chopped**

Bathe this mixture in sufficient olive oil and toss lightly to mix. Add sufficient herb seasoning to taste plus:

Juice of 1 lemon

Parsnips are best purchased in the winter time after the first frost. This mellows and sweetens their flavor.

[1] *You may substitute salsify or oyster plant. However, salsify should be steamed first for about 10 minutes.*

[2] *If fresh parsley is not available, substitute ¼ cup dried parsley.*

For added joy, throw in some crushed garlic cloves and mix thoroughly with the olive oil.

PARSLEY LEMON BUTTER
4 Servings

Take:

½ cup butter

and cream slightly softened butter, adding:

2 tablespoons fresh lemon juice

as it becomes pliable. Then add:

- **1 teaspoon herb seasoning or sea salt**
- **A pinch of cayenne pepper**
- **1 tablespoon finely minced parsley**

Seasoned butters may be frozen for several weeks. However, they should not be refrigerated longer than 24 hours since the herbs deteriorate quickly.

AUNT EFFIE . . .
Cousin Lulubelle is concerned about her facial blemishes!

Nature gives you the face you have at twenty; it is up to her to merit the face she has at forty! That woman is one of the Lee sisters and her first name is Ug. I never forget a face, but I'm willing to make an exception in her case. Cousin Lulubelle only seems to put on weight in certain places . . . pizza parlors, bakeries and ice cream shops.

Lulubelle oughta start eating that parsley and pushing the bacon and eggs aside if she's concerned about her face. I take a handful of fresh parsley, boil it in one pint of water for 10 minutes. Then I wash my face with this solution every morning upon arising and every evening before going to bed. It should be made fresh daily. I noticed an improvement in my complexion within one week! If she takes a handful of parsley and boils it in one quart of water . . . making a broth . . . taking a few ounces at a time during the day, Lulubelle will find this will solve her "monthly" problems giving her smooth menstrual flow. And the same concoction is good for gout, arthritis, kidney stones, pinworms and gallbladder disorders. Tell her to take 2 cups daily before meals.

15

CAPTURING THE CHARISMA OF COMFREY

**Getting
Rid of an
Earache**

We were away from home. I was on a speaking tour giving health seminars in major cities. My son was accompanying me. He had left home with an earache. It got progessively worse on the trip. Quite fortunately we had several tea bags of comfrey with us. So I suggested he pour hot water over the tea bag, let it steep, then drink half the tea and pour the rest over a washcloth and let that effusion drip slowly in his ear . . . keeping the solution in his ear all night.

He awoke the next morning his earache all gone!

We were in Kansas City this past summer. My wife had a cold plus an earache. Again we were fortunate to have one tea bag of comfrey. I suggested the same procedure. She awoke the next day with her earache all gone!

Comfrey is a versatile herb. Those who are aware of comfrey know its many valuable properties when illness strikes. Those who are not familiar with comfrey . . . when told of its healing abilities . . . often look at you with comic disbelief!

The Perils of Little Annie

Little Annie has a cold today
And Annie's mother knows
That Annie needs a dose of drugs
To clear that runny nose.

Little Annie has another cold
And now her throat's so sore
That Annie's mother gets the bottle out
To give her a few ounces more.

Little Annie's feeling sluggish now
And her nose is blocked and red.
Her mother gets her an antibiotic
And sends her straight to bed.

Little Annie's head is really hot
And her throat is really sore.
Little Annie goes to the hospital
Now her tonsils are no more!

Little Annie's grandmom came today
And gave her Comfrey tea.
Little Annie's all better now . . .
And the Doctor said:
     "It's the medicine, you see!"

Salem Kirban

Throughout the centuries comfrey has been used in poultices made from the leaves to reduce swellings, to teas or infusions used to treat diarrhea.

In the Herb Hall of Fame

I can remember at the retreat in Blue Ridge, Georgia that Dr. Carey Reams had quite a large garden of comfrey plants. He used comfrey as a principal item in Green Drink (vegetable drink). Its primary purpose was to drive the sugar level down for those people with high sugars. This Green Drink is only given if the sugar reading (on the Reams scale of measurement) is 5.50 or higher.

Comfrey is a member of the Forget-me-not tribe of herbs. And anyone who has used it is not likely to forget its many benefits.

Comfrey has been called knitbone, knitback, healing herb and slippery root. Comfrey can be classified as one of the ten most practical herbs in existence.

Used For Mending Broken Bones

The Greeks were using comfrey as long as three thousand years ago! Comfrey was a popular remedy for mending broken bones and battle wounds in the Middle Ages. It was there that it was given the name "knitbone" because of its remarkable ability to reduce swelling around fractures and to promote bone union.

They also used it as a remedy for bleeding hemorrhoids and for persistent coughts and lung problems.

The people of Ireland have used comfrey for centuries to strengthen the blood and for circulation problems.

Comfrey contains a most important ingredient called

allantoin

Helps Heal Ulcers

Allantoin is considered a cell proliferant. Proliferant means to "reproduce new parts in quick succession." Because of this it has been used to strengthen skin tissue and help in the healing of ulcers.

Dr. Charles J. Macalister, an English physician, observed the benefits of comfrey in various medical cases he treated over the years. In 1936 he wrote a book on the subject.

Dr. Macalister noted that allantoin is present in the urine of pregnant women and also in their maternal milk. He concluded that somehow allantoin must be related to the process of growth and the multiplication of cells.

He also noted that allantoin is available in large amounts to the fetus in the earliest months of pregnancy. It then gradually diminishes as the pregnancy progresses. He then checked out the comfrey plant and noted that from January to March the rhizome (small creeping root usually growing horizontally just under the surface) contains a very high proportion of allantoin . . . about 8/10ths of 1 per cent. A few months later this drops to 4/10ths of 1 per cent. And by summer there is no noticeable amount of allantoin in the root structure of the comfrey but instead, it is discoverable in the leaves and buds of the plant. Here it is used for cell-proliferation.

Dr. Macalister, further intrigued by this mystery plant, then injected a solution of allantoin into bulbs of other plants. He noted that when he did this, they grew much more rapidly than plants that were not treated!

**An
Unusual
Healing
Liquid**

He then began to use allantoin in treating pneumonia patients. He would have them drink an oral solution of the precious healing liquid. Soon he discovered that the patients in his ward who received allantoin had a mortality rate 75% lower than patients who did not receive this!

From the early days of England, folklore has been maintained that comfrey is useful in fighting cancer. Scientific tests have not been able to confirm this but some admit that benefits from comfrey are noteworthy.

**The
New Zealand
Nibble**

The New Zealanders believe comfrey is a miracle working plant. It is not unusual to find them nibbling on the comfrey leaf like many Americans would nibble on potato chips. One individual who had been suffering from asthma for 30 years started chewing on comfrey quite accidently. That night he had his first night of unbroken sleep. He couldn't understand why. He was used to restless, fatiguing nights.

Checking his previous day's activities he recalled that the only thing he did that was apart from routine was chewing on a comfrey leaf. He decided to follow this routine daily and his asthma disappeared. Many report they sleep better, eat better and feel fitter once they start nibbling comfrey.

Throughout the centuries comfrey has been taken by people suffering from asthma, eczema, digestive disorders, arthritis, varicose ulcers and other health problems.

A Healing Herb

But, of course, as I mentioned earlier such a solution to health problems is too simplistic. And only the simple would believe that herbs have any healing power.

Perhaps that's why I am simple. Being simple means that something is uncomplicated, easy to do or to understand.

Comfrey is an herb. And herbs are mentioned at least 32 times in the Bible. As early as Genesis 1:11, in the creation, God created three important types of vegetation:

> And God said,
> *Let the earth bring forth grass,*
> *the herb yielding seed,*
> *and the fruit tree yielding fruit . . .*

My First Comfrey Plant

It was only after 50 years of age that I became acquainted with the comfrey plant. A friend of mine, Charles W. Ollard, who runs a stationery store in Southampton, Pennsylvania, quite often discusses his garden with me. One day I asked him about comfrey and he told me he had numerous plants in his garden and just "couldn't get rid of it." He told me how hardy the plant was and grew in spite of lack of any care. I gladly accepted two plants and put them in among my roses. They have been growing profusely ever since.

My associate, Bob Conner, decided he wanted a comfrey plant. I got several from Mr. Ollard and let them sit on the back lawn in a bag. When Bob left later that day to drive back to his home in Massachusetts he forgot to take the comfrey plants. I had to go out of town on a speaking tour and there they sat in a partially closed shopping bag during the hottest part of the summer.

**The
Hardy
Comfrey**

When I finally discovered the forgotten comfrey, they were black and wilted. I thought they were dead. But, knowing of comfrey's remarkable abilities, I was determined to put them to a test. I planted the "dead" plants in pots and left them on the lawn after watering them thoroughly. In a week or so some green shoots appeared. The dead plant had come back to life. Bob finally, about one month later, got them transplanted in his Massachusetts garden and they are thriving!

The comfrey can be considered somewhat of a resurrection plant. It certainly is hardy and thrives in all types of weather and, in spite of mishandling. Comfrey roots can withstand temperatures as low as 40° below zero.

**The
Secret of
Comfrey**

The precious ingredient, allantoin, is concentrated in the surface roots in winter and early spring. Then the new leaves and shoots contain the greatest quantity during the summer.

Many people use the new, tender leaves in their salads. The leaves are slightly fuzzy so it is best to chop them into tiny pieces.

Allantoin is very sensitive to alkalies. That is why when you are using comfrey in a healing preparation, use only distilled water. Allantoin is sensitive to the alkalies present in tap water. Also, never boil the water which contains comfrey. This can destroy the precious ingredient, allantoin! Also, it is best to make solutions of comfrey every day when using as a poultice or other application. Older solutions lose their effectiveness.

How To Harvest

It is best to harvest comfrey just before it blooms. Many believe that the nutritional and medicinal value of comfrey decreases after the blooming period for that year. Those knowledgeable in herbs prefer to use the fresh comfrey rather than the dried leaves.

Comfrey is high in calcium, phosphorus and potassium. It is also rich in Vitamins A and C. Those who like to bake will be interested in knowing that comfrey leaves can be dried, ground and added to bread or muffins. It is rich in Vitamin B_{12}. While Vitamin B_{12} has long been known for its value in treating pernicious anemia, many are also recognizing its benefits to the brain and nervous system.[1] Comfrey is the only land plant that contains this important Vitamin!

Those who bask under the charisma of the comfrey know that it is a plant of many virtues. It is one of nature's healing grasses. Anyone can grow this hardy herb in their backyard. Most everyone has a medicine cabinet loaded with headache tablets, cold pills with those multiple tiny time capsules ready to explode at various intervals, antidiarrhea liquids and bottles of pink antacid. Such a variety puts quite a strain on one's

[1] Carlton Fredericks, Ph.D., Look Younger, Feel Healthier (New York: Grosset & Dunlap), 1972, pp. 120-124.

pocketbook and, more important, on one's human system.

Nature's Drugstore

Instead, why not plant a comfrey plant. It is nature's drugstore. Once you, too, capture the charisma of comfrey, you will glow in its warmth of well-being and inner healing. You may never see an eggplant smile, but if comfrey becomes part of your life, chances are you will smile more often!

COMFREY/CELERY JUICE DRINK
Six 8-ounce Glasses

For a different, refreshing and most nourishing drink, mix the following ingredients in a bowl:

- **2-3 cups young tender comfrey leaves washed, drained and chopped**
- **¼ cup celery leaves chopped**
- **1 small onion chopped**
- **½ cup shredded escarole**
- **1 fresh pear, cored and chopped**
- **4 mint leaves**

Place one-half cup of the greens mixture into an electric blender with one-quarter cup of apple cider and blend. Repeat this procedure until entire mixture is blended into a drinkable consistency. You may add additional apple cider if necessary. For greater aliveness, stir in:

Juice of 1 lemon

You may season with honey to taste, if you wish.

If you have a juicer there is no need to chop ingredients . . . just feed into juicer and mix with sufficient apple cider. Or, better still, run apples through your juicer to make fresh apple juice.

COMFREY RAINBOW SALAD
6 Servings

Comfrey is very easy to grow. It is best to eat or juice the young, tender leaves. Comfrey leaves are furry on the back and may tickle your palate. In making this salad, you may wish to lightly steam the comfrey. Then drain very well and place in frige to crisp up. Now, you are ready for a real treat! Take:

Comfrey leaves
(Sufficient to make salad for 6 people) and chop and place in bowl

To this add:

- **1 small zucchini squash diced**
- **1 tomato chopped**
- **1 cucumber diced**
- **3 radishes diced
  (and radish tops chopped)**
- **2 scallions chopped**
- **1 stalk celery chopped**

Mix well and moisten generously with your favorite dressing. Mine is olive oil. Also squeeze on the entire salad:

Juice of 1 fresh lemon

Mix again and, if you dare, add:

Garlic powder lightly dusted
A tinche of cayenne pepper

Top each serving with a pepper ring with a cherry tomato in the center. Don't forget to add any herb seasoning to sparkle salad or at least have it on the table for your guests to select.

AUNT EFFIE . . .
Have you seen Cora Mae's varicose veins lately?

No! And I don't expect anyone else wants to see them either. She has a disposition that needs repositioning. Doctors claim that cheerful people resist diseases much better than glum ones. Cora Mae oughta remember it's "the surly bird that always catches the germ."

The oddest thing happened the other day in her house. The clock fell off the wall, and if it had fallen a moment sooner it would have hit her mother. Cora Mae's husband always did say that clock was slow. Honestly, Cora Mae doesn't have an ounce of common sense. If fish is brain food, she better eat a whale.

She wears tight girdles that bind her tummy and high fashioned boots that bind her legs and eats cakes, pies and candy that bind her bowels. No wonder she has varicose veins!

Look at Granny Osgood. Her legs are as supple as the dew on a blade of grass! When she had varicose veins, she would take the tender leaves of comfrey, run them through a blender so they were chopped up fine, then place this poultice on the veins overnight, wrapped with a washcloth. The swelling went down, and the pain disappeared. She even put the poultice on an ulcer and it disappeared. She mixed a fresh brew each day. Now she drinks comfrey tea and eats sensibly.

16

HOW TO BE JOYFUL . . .
WHEN THERE'S NOTHING TO BE HAPPY ABOUT!

We live in a stress environment!

In the last few years, through my travels around the United States and Canada, I have noticed that the mood of the people is changing.

Fellowship has turned into fear. Graces have turned to grumbles. Joy has turned to jeering. Accolades have turned to anger. Love has turned to lawsuits.

Times Have Changed

We spend more time being concerned about oil on a duck's back than we do about the pollution of some television shows on a child's mind. We spend more time fighting for more government handouts than we do for sensible nutritious lunches for our children while at school.

When I was a child, and was called into the principal's office, I was the one that was quaking in my boots. Today it is different! When a child goes into the principal's office, the principal is quaking in his boots . . . as the child is accompanied by his two lawyers!

Most people have lost the secret of tranquil, peaceful living. We are slaves to time. God had infinite time to give us. But how did He give it? In one immense millennium? No. He carefully divided it up in an orderly succession of new mornings, new afternoons, new sundowns and new evenings. Twenty-four hours of day broken into 4 segments whose changes are (at the moment of change) barely perCeptible. Amazing.

Man's Tragedy With Time

Along comes man and he is not content with this separation of time. Hundreds of years ago he decided to further divide it into hours, using a sundial. But at that point, the pace of life was still slow.

Then came so-called modern technology and along came the grandfather clock which broke time down into hours and minutes. Still the pace was not too hectic. One could sit in a rocking chair and listen to the ticking of the clock, and the melodious ringing of the chimes at the 15-minute or half-hour cycle. At this stage time and activity was not measured by 4 changes (dawn, afternoon, sundown and evening). Instead it was measured by at least 24 changes; that is 24 hours.

Science, still not satisfied with God's way of planning the universe, sought new "improvements."

Along came the watch with its sweep second hand that not only measured hours and minutes but also measured seconds. Again man readjusted to this further refinement of time. It was apparent that he was becoming a slave to time. What he was forgetting was that:

> An inch of time on the sundial
> is worth more than 12 inches of jade!

In man's desire to gain more material possessions he was losing his most valued earthly possession - TIME.

TIMELY THOUGHTS ON TIME

A child was overheard meditating aloud: "At Grandmamma's there isn't any We-don't-have-time-to-do-that ... Grandmamma doesn't have a watch on her arm. ... At Grandmamma's I feel good."

* * *

Your calendar shows the passing of time. Your face shows what you are doing with it.

* * *

Time has no divisions to mark its passage; there is never a thunderstorm or blare of trumpets to announce the beginning of a new year. Even when a new century begins, it is only we mortals who ring bells and fire off pistols.

* * *

All my possessions for a moment of time.
Queen Elizabeth I's last words

* * *

Time is too slow for those who Wait,
        too swift for those who Fear,
        too long for those who Grieve,
        too short for those who Rejoice.

* * *

How do you spend your time? If you live to be seventy, chances are you will spend at least 20 years asleep, 10 years watching television and 10 years eating, 4 years driving back and forth to work, 6 years *"killing time"* waiting in lines and participating in frivolous amusements. The balance of about 20 solid years will be in working so you can retire and have *"time on your hands"* to enjoy life.

* * *

And chances are, you already have tomorrow segmented off not in hours, but in half-hours and minutes and in moments ... from the moment you awaken until you retire that evening. Don't be a slave to earthly time. Place your priorities for time with eternity's values in view.

Then came the ultimate of all ultimates . . . the marvelous discoveries of time in the 1970's . . . the digital watch. Now, not only can we tell the time, but we can make it light up. Now, not only can we measure seconds . . . we can measure tenth's of a second!

How Time Was Polluted

And what do we do with this precious time that God gave to us in 4 segments that we have now broken down into first,

> 24 hour segments,
> > then into
> 1440 minutes segments,
> > then into
> 86,400 second segments,
> > and now into
> 864,000 tenth of a second segments!

My what marvelous progress we've made that we can capture so much time . . . from God's 4 segments to man's 864,000 segments in one day!

If time is so important to us that we have achieved this minute segmentation then how do we appropriate it?

A Race Against Time

We get up in the morning and race through a meal of tea and toast or coffee and a doughnut. And if we are more sophisticated we have a glass of artificial orange juice and a sugary cereal. Then we hop into our car and spend anywhere from 1/2 hour to an hour battling thousands of other motorists in a nerve-racking race to get to the office. In the meantime we fill our environment with fumes and (if we were calm when we started) the irritations of driving turn us into a monster.

**The
Pressure
Cooker
We Call
Life**

We spend the morning sitting around in an office that more resembles a pressure cooker. Instead of steam, however, we breathe a pure mixture of cigarette smoke. Our tranquility is constantly jangled by the telephone. Our fellow workers, molded in the same "slave of time slot," do not flow by us as a gentle river but seem to grate against our own personality. The strive for position, for material possessions, turns fairly rational human beings into irritable, scheming, feuding individuals.

Now comes the lunch break! If time is precious, we gulp down a soggy bologna sandwich and wash it down with a soft drink or coffee then top it off with a cigarette in our mouth and a telephone in our ear.

If we are in the executive capacity, we dine out, starting first with a pre-lunch cocktail, then settle down to a thick, rare steak, coffee and pie or ice cream. To ease the pressure, we down a Valium.

Back to the office to work and we feel a headache coming on, so we take an aspirin. Then it is back to the freeway in a race that resembles the Grand Prix without prizes! Every minute . . . every second counts.

We get home, gulp down dinner and slump in front of the TV for 3 or 4 hours, then eat a late snack and collapse into bed.

For the housewife, the schedule is a little different. She never has enough hours in the day. She is not master of most of her time. Much of her time is robbed from her.

After hustling the children to school, she has to see the doctor. He makes the appointment for 11 AM. She gets there on time and sits, and sits, and sits! He finally takes her at 1 PM and spends 5 minutes with her. He gives her a prescription and she has just gone through about $15 to $20 and lost at least 2 hours.

The Perils Of Motherhood

Then she remembers a dental appointment at 2. She gets there at 2 PM and sits, and sits and sits. He takes her at 2:45, takes x-rays for $20 and tells her she needs root canal work at $200. She exits at 3:45 some $220 poorer, anticipating the stress that will be generated when she breaks the news to her husband.

She remembers there is no food for dinner. So, she stops at the supermarket to pick up four TV dinners and some soft drinks. Fortunately the supermarket has a express line. She stands in the express line with about 15 other people, but they have installed a new computer to generate speed. Gone are the old days when a girl simply punched a key on the cash register and handed you your change . . . all within 10 seconds. Now, each product has a code. She must punch several code keys.

Is it a dairy product or a vegetable?
Is it taxable or non-taxable?
Are you paying with food stamps or with cash?
(And if cash, WHY?)
Are you using discount coupons or not?

Then she starts to punch the code numbers and the price. Suddenly she stops. It's her break time ... *"Sorry, you'll have to go to another counter, my union says I am to have 5 breaks a day plus 2 coffee breaks."*

**Headed
For A
Nervous
Breakdown**

And if that doesn't occur, then the computer tape breaks or the machine refuses to function. Her express line that was supposed to process her in one minute ends up taking 15. More frazzled nerves.

The children come home from school, wound up like a clock, after having ingested the school lunch of additives and colon cloggers. They either plant themselves at the idiot box (TV) or raid the cookie box to get some snack. (Last year Americans gobbled almost 2 billion cookies adding $3.5 billion to the coffers of the snack food industry!)

Dad comes home from work for a sumptious TV dinner and is bombarded with the problems of wife and children ... listening to the plaintive demands from their teenage daughter that she *"just must have her own car and private telephone"* because *"... all the kids do, and I'll be weird!"*

So the day goes. Dad, racing every minute of the day, grasping every second of time and headed for hypertension (high blood pressure), a stroke or a heart attack at 42. Mom, wanting to take advantage of time, but finding others squandering her time, and headed for a nervous breakdown.

What has happened to our lives?

Why do we become slaves to a stress environment?

This complex civilization confronts us with many more monumental problems than our forefathers faced. Yet, how can we be joyful when, on the surface there appears nothing to be joyful about?

Lose Yourself

I know that some people who give advice on living in a stress environment say that first, you must FIND YOURSELF. And there is much truth to that. But, on the other hand, perhaps also you must **LOSE YOURSELF.**

Now this may be hard to do. But stand back for a day or an hour and lose yourself in quiet reflection taking inventory of your life.

Seeking Solutions

I did this some 3000 miles away from home in October, 1977. That month of October was perhaps the most stressful month I have ever lived through. Two nights I did not sleep. I tossed and turned and was in almost constant prayer to God asking Him to guide me and give me wisdom. I was trying to do too many things in my own strength and ingenuity. And the things I accomplished were successful. But some of my decisions were wrong ones. And some things went wrong that were outside of my control. But they were still my problems. I had to, through God, turn them into solutions.

What caused the stress ... the sleepless nights? I had financial obligations of some $30,000 that had to be resolved in about a week's time. And my bank account at the time was so low it reminded me of the parable of the 5 loaves and 2 fishes that were available to feed some 5000 people!

Isn't that enough to cause anyone not only stress but DISTRESS!

A Wonderful Combination

No wonder I couldn't sleep. But I discovered something amazing. Even though I had sleepless nights, I could awake refreshed and alive in the morning full of energy. The reason: I **first** put my trust in God to meet my needs and **second,** I was following a sound program of nutrition.

Doesn't it always happen that when your income is low, suddenly everyone and their brother needs to be paid immediately? It seems that way.

Anyway . . . I had stress, plenty of it. At that moment, I had so much stress, I would not have minded sharing it with someone else. I reasoned, **"Dear Lord, why should I be blessed with all this stress, when some people hardly have any? Can't we spread it around a bit?"**

Count It All Joy

I carry a pocket Bible when I travel. So I picked it up and asked the Lord to show me some promise verses. And He did! At first I was amazed at what they said:

My brethren,
*count it all **joy***
when you encounter
various trials.

(James 1:2 NAS)

What? Count it all **JOY?** How can I be joyful when I've got to come up with $30,000. How can I be joyful, when I have to finish writing the last two chapters of *THE GETTING BACK TO NATURE DIET* . . . then somehow gather some extra $10,000 together to get the book printed? How can I be joyful when The College of Physicians and Surgeons issued injunctions against me in Toronto and Regina prohibiting me from giving a health lecture? How? **How can I be joyful . . . when there is NOTHING to be joyful about!**

Boy, was I stressful! In my lectures I had been telling others how to find peace . . . but now I had no peace. JOY? It's easy to be joyful when everything is going fine . . . there is money in the bank. But how can one be joyful when everything is going WRONG?

The Secret To Living

Then I remembered what I had told many church congregations and those who attended my health seminars:

> *Be still*
> *and know that I am God . . .*
>
> (Psalm 46:10 KJV)

"Be still." How hard it is to be still, when I feel I have to DO SOMETHING to resolve the problem.

Be still.

What does it mean?

In the Bible it means:

> **Cease from striving!**
> **RELAX!**

Then, God, in His tenderness showed me another verse in the Old Testament book of Psalms . . . a verse that changed my life that day:

> *Our soul waiteth for the Lord:*
> *He is our help and our shield.*
>
> (Psalm 33:20 KJV)

I can't explain the miracles of God. All I can tell you is that a miracle happened in my life.

I became a new person. My entire perspective changed. Alone, 3000 miles away from home, in quietness on the Canadian prairies of Alberta, at Prairie Bible Institute, God turned me around and I could see and understand how my life should be lived.

My Life Was Changed

You may find this hard to believe. But from that day on . . . although I was under unbelievable stress . . . I had complete peace of mind and a new JOY. Normally, I would be beside myself with nervous tension, taking tranquilizers or headache pills, jumpy and trying to work out everything myself. But things were different now. Something really happened to me!

I am writing this chapter on Wednesday, November 3, 1977. Some of the conditions that caused the stress are still there but I still have that calm assurance, that peace of mind, and that joy. And I wouldn't trade it for anything.

Also, I have seen God work. I was determined that I would put everything in His hands. The $30,000? That indebtedness is now whittled down to about $10,000 already. And in this past few days I have witnessed miracle after miracle.

We worry too much. We really should not worry at all!

A Lesson To Learn

I remember the story about the Grandfather clock. A young new clock was placed next to him on the shelf of the clockmaker's store. The young clock was anxious and most nervous, fretting with his hands. The old Grandfather clock asked him why he was so troubled.

The young clock said:

I am so worried.
I have to tick 24 hours a day.
I have to tick 1440 minutes a day.
I have to tick 86,400 seconds a day.
I just don't know how I am ever going
to accomplish this!

The Grandfather clock, looking compassionately at the young new clock said:

**All you have to do, son,
is TICK
ONE TICK AT A TIME!**

**Three
Guidelines
To
Happiness**

How can you be joyful when there is nothing
to be joyful about:

1. Relax

Cease from striving in your own
might! Place your foundation in
God.

2. Realign your priorities

What areas are causing you stress
situations? Is it because your family
is so engulfed in grasping material
things and shunting spiritual values? Are you so engrossed in your
own selfish desires and goals that
you fail to communicate love and
concern for others in your family?
Realign your priorities. It may be
more important for you and your
wife to take a walk around the
block every evening, holding
hands, rather than watching TV or
working overtime at the office.

3. Realign your goals

Write down on a piece of paper your goals. Break it down into 4 categories.

1. My goals for this week
2. My goals for this month
3. My goals for this year
4. My long range goals for my life

Now, next to those goals you spell out, take time to honestly grade them. Will achieving each of those goals bring you happiness, peace of mind, a united family, a harmonious marriage, and a rich, spiritual life? If so, those goals are worthy of pursuit.

On the other hand, will those goals simply help you gain more material possessions, a raise in pay, a promotion at the office, more committees to serve on or more clothes or physical beauty? If so, you should seriously consider what direction you are headed.

Some women are so slow they take an hour to make a pot of instant coffee. But this is good! We are living in a world that demands INSTANT.

**Get Back
To A
Slower Pace**

We drink INSTANT coffee. We eat INSTANT mashed potatoes. We take our cars to a MINUTE car wash. When we are depressed we take a Valium to get INSTANT release. When we have a cold or infection, we rush to get an antibiotic to get INSTANT healing. When we cook rice we use MINUTE rice. When we cook cereal we look for MINUTE oatmeal. We tend to attend churches that give us CAPSULED sermons. Many states, in the erroneous belief that gambling can resolve problems, now make available INSTANT lotteries. When we watch football on television we are bombarded with INSTANT replay.

No wonder it appears that one half of the world is neurotic and the other half is tranquilized.

How To Avoid The Perils Of Stress

Of course we live in a stress environment. But we do not have to allow the stress circumstances around us to control our lives! And that's the secret in a nutshell!

My wife and I heard a memorable sermon some 25 years ago where the Pastor reminded the congregation:

> *Don't let someone else's attitude affect yours!*

You can live with stress if you RELAX, REALIGN YOUR PRIORITIES and REALIGN YOUR GOALS.

Three Guidelines For Contentment

If you have already placed your faith in the Word of God you are given three guideposts for peace and joy:

1. **Delight** yourself in the Lord;
   And He will give you the desires
   of your heart.

2. **Commit** your way to the Lord,

3. **Trust** also in Him,
   and He will do it!

   (Psalm 37:4-5 NAS)

Delight . . . Commit . . . Trust. Are you ready

to find joy . . . even when there appears to be nothing to be joyful about? Are you ready to sail through the storms of stress as though you were on a sea of tranquility? I wish mere words could convey to you the exhilarating, stimulating, live-giving joy that is found when you take God at His Word!

Now Is The Time!

Are you willing to make this change in your own life? Not next week, not tomorrow, but right now?

I challenge you to get back to God's nature . . . to find the joy that will make you a new person. By finding it, you will take the distress out of stress and every problem will have a solution!

17

WHAT IS THE "GETTING BACK TO NATURE" DIET?

Nature. That's a big word which can mean many things to different people. But, basically, getting back to nature is actually getting back to the simple way of life; in all facets of life.

Let me give you an illustration that may help.

A few years ago I was stranded at the Chicago O'Hare airport because of a snowstorm. The airport was virtually closed for two days. Thousands of people were milling around the terminal waiting for flights to resume. Why the delay in clearing the airport? It took almost a day and a half for the snow removal equipment just to get to the airport to clear the runways! The sophistication of mechanization!

Discover The Simple Things Of Life

Now, in China, when a snowstorm hits a major airport, they employ a different technique. They line up 500 or so Chinese on the runway and place in their hands a marvelous "new" invention. It is called a shovel. And they have the runway cleared in a few hours!

In Chicago it now takes **4** people to change a light bulb in the city streets. One carries the ladder, one carries the bulb, another puts the bulb into the socket and the fourth person is the foreman. Four people to change a light bulb and it costs the city about $232 per light bulb change!

In the United States, as well as in many countries, we have gone far beyond the realm of common sense approaches to problems and the basic guidelines provided in nature.

Do We Need More Drugs?

Medical doctors are concerned about the length of time it takes to get a new drug approved. In 1966, it took 35 months. Now it takes over 96 months (8 years). But the question must be asked . . . do we need new drugs, or do we need to examine our values and strive to get back to nature. Many practitioners believe the present drugs available are adequate to meet most needs. Perhaps greater effort should be made in researching the natural approach to health rather than seeking new pills for assorted ills.

The Nutritional Approach

If a housewife of 30 years of age entered a doctor's office and complained about nervousness and headaches, she would most likely walk out with a prescription for a Valium-type drug. But August Daro, M.D., believes in applying the back-to-nature approach to health problems. He placed this woman on a supplement containing magnesium, calcium and vitamin D. He gave the same recommendations for a 38-year-old woman who had been plagued all her adult life with premenstrual tension and severe cramps during her period. She was completely relieved.[1]

How To Be Happy

The Getting Back To Nature Diet incorporates **three BE's.** The first **BE** is in this chapter.

If we can make sure these **three BE's** are a daily part of our life, we will have come a long way to a happier and healthier life.

[1] The Doctor Who Takes His Own Medicine (Penna: Prevention), October, 1977, p. 55.

1. BE POSITIVE

Now to accomplish that takes a little work. Let's take myself, for example. This is the last chapter I am writing in this book (although numerically, it is not the last, for I don't always write chapters in the sequence they will appear). I saved this chapter for the last because it is the most difficult for me to write. Now, normally, I should have tackled the most difficult chapter first, but I just was not sure exactly how I was going to approach this subject and wanted time for it to formulate in my mind. Now I know the approach I am going to take.

Overcoming Objections

But that doesn't get the chapter written! In fact, there is no <u>earthly</u> reason why I should be positive today as I write this chapter. Let me tell you why.

1. **It is raining.**
   And it has been raining
   for the past 3 days
   and the weather man promises rain
   for the next 6 days.
2. **It is early in the morning**
   and my mind is occupied
   with a thousand and one things
   I just have to do!
3. **I've got to resolve some financial hurdles** to keep our organization running smoothly.

Now, what in the world is there to be positive about!

Yet the first step to good health is **BE POSI-**

In 1967 I took my first round-the-world trip investigating world conditions. I remember flying into Amman, Jordan and driving outside the city to the barren desert. There, in the middle of nowhere was an Arab refugee camp. The family pictured above had lost everything which represented about $2500 in property and goods. They asked me to sit down and drink Turkish coffee with them. I walked inside their tent to see what possessions they had brought with them. All I found were a couple pots and pans, a little coffee pot and four tiny coffee cups — from which they humbly served me.

I had eaten in opulent restaurants, spotlessly clean. But now, as the sand whipped across our faces . . . I felt at home. Here was humble truth unvarnished by the glittering selfishness of the world. I would not have traded that experience for anything.

For them, they did not measure time in hours, nor in days, nor in months. They measured time in years.

They were pawns in the middle of an Arab-Israeli conflict. There would be no easy solution to their problem. Yet that family had an inner peace and calm. Although, by this world's standards, they had nothing; their positive outlook on life gave them a joy beyond price.

**Be A
Part of
The Solution**

TIVE. That doesn't mean you cannot be negative. Of course you can! But be negative in a POSITIVE WAY! I would estimate that 98% of Americans are bogged down by problems. The successful 2% are aware of their problems but seek solutions. Are you a part of the problem or are you part of the solution?

Don't say: *"Boy, am I feeling dragged out today!"* (negative)

Instead say: *"Boy, am I feeling dragged out today! (negative)
My body is trying to tell me something. (transition)
And I'm going to do something about it!"* (positive action)

The difference is all in the approach!

You can have the best medical treatment that physicians have to offer. You can be following the best natural approach to health that nutritionists recommend. You can faithfully take vitamin and mineral supplements, go on a fast and drink distilled water . . . and still feel miserable!

**Mental
Attitude
Is
Important**

Why? Because of your negative mental attitude. As Dr. John L. Black so aptly puts it:

*A team of well-fed horses
    can race wildly over a cliff
    just as easily as
A team of half-starved horses.*

Spirit, soul and body must be in perfect harmony. During the course of our research on the Carey Reams urine/saliva nutrition program, I met many people whose entire approach to health was negative. Pessimism (or negativism) is that practice of looking on the dark side of things; the tendency to expect misfortune or the worst outcome in any circumstance. I am sure you remember the saying:

> *My mother told me to cheer up*
> *because things could be worse.*
>
> *So I cheered up and*
> *things did get worse.*

Don't Be A Pessimist

That's pessimism! There is no one with so gloomy an outlook as the pessimist who dreads the evil day when things get better. A pessimist avoids looking at the bright side of things out of fear of getting eyestrain.

Pessimists are all alike: they are always good for bad news. The pessimist can't enjoy his health today because he may be sick tomorrow. There is nothing like happiness for making a pessimist unhappy. A pessimist not only expects the worst, but makes the worst of it when it happens.

To the pessiment . . .
life is just a pile of dirty dishes.

To the optimist . . .
life is a continuing banquet!

BE POSITIVE!

The Bible is filled with illustrations of those who looked on life with a pessimistic view. The children of Israel, during the great exodus into the Promised Land, are a prime example.

1. They complained asking Moses: *"Who will give us meat to eat?"* (Numbers 11:4)

2. They complained because they could not secure fish, cucumbers, melons, leeks, onions and garlic like they had in Egypt. (Numbers 11:5)

3. They complained because their appetite had left them. (Numbers 11:6)

4. They complained about their leadership. (Numbers 12:1)

5. They complained because the Promised Land had giants that made the Israelities look small as grasshoppers. (Numbers 13:32-33)

Count Your Blessings

Is it no wonder Moses wanted to die rather than face this continual grumbling and murmuring! His people had too quickly forgotten the miraculous crossing of the Red Sea and their freedom from the bondage of Egypt!

The first step to good health in GETTING BACK TO NATURE is to BE POSITIVE!

Today is Monday. It is raining. I am not in the mood for writing this chapter. But, as I do with every chapter, I first sit at the typewriter and pray, asking God to guide my thoughts. That is positive! I then put a sheet of paper in the typewriter. That is positive! I then started to type! That is positive. And ideas did come to me and a continual flow of thought.

Get Started

How easy it would have been to say, "I've got so many other details to do, and today is such a miserable day, I'll just postpone writing this chapter and get involved in all the other odds and ends." That is negative! And if I kept up that approach, you would never be reading this book. Because there never would be a book!

BE POSITIVE!

A pessimist looks at sunshine as something that casts shadows.

18

HOW TO WALK THE PATH OF BETTER HEALTH

The second **BE** along the path to a healthier and happier you is:

2. BE SELECTIVE

We are eating too much and we are eating the wrong kinds of food. It was Dr. Paul Dudley White who said:

> *We were born, really, to be field animals. To rise with the sun . . . to eat only when hunger dictates.*

Don't Be Fooled

This statement is worthy of consideration. We are not selective in the foods that we eat. The housewife is bombarded with over 10,000 slickly packaged products in her supermarket . . . all cleverly designed to capture her attention. It is called subliminal seduction.

Subliminal means a compelling force that is created below your threshold of consciousness. This is done by repetition via such things as television and radio commercials and newspaper ads. It is done by package design and wording, creating a stimuli that will trigger a response as you pass that package. **And you do it not really being fully conscious of your actions!**

AVOID THESE FOODS

Pancakes

Sausage Links

Bacon

Fried Chicken

Fried Shrimp

French Fries

Pork Chops

Ham

Hot Dogs

Ice Cream

Advertising agencies have been known to place hidden cameras behind their products in a supermarket. The cameras are designed to photograph your eyes as you pass the shelf in question. If your "blink-rate" slows down, the advertiser knows that his package design is effective and that it has momentarily hypnotized you. Chances are good that you will select that product. (Of course, as you see the cash register jangle up that enormous bill, your blink-rate flutters frantically . . . but it's too late, you've been hooked.)

BE SELECTIVE IN THE FOOD YOU EAT! The major degenerative diseases, heart disease and atherosclerosis, are caused primarily by the kind of food we eat.

A Better Diet Can Actually Save You Money!

For the most part, the American housewife determines the diet for her entire family. She wouldn't dream of pushing her 3-year-old child into the path of a speeding automobile! Yet she will allow him to eat a sugary cereal for breakfast, and a fast-food-fare restaurant hamburger on a colon-clogging bun and french fries and a cola for lunch. Then she will top his evening snack with a candy bar or potato chips. The car is a fast death . . . the diet is a slow death, but perhaps a more agonizing one.

For, continuing on this diet, the child may be faced with a multiplicity of growing diseases. He may be plagued with the silent diseases of fatigue, plus a lack of purpose, a growing irritability, a hyperactive condition that make it impossible for him to concentrate on anything, a distortion of priorities in life, or a lack of lasting goals. And most sad, he will pass on these qualities to his wife and children. And for them, the fight for sanity will be an uphill one!

Getting hit by a car is dramatic and initially devastating. Slowly eating a poisonous diet is far more subtle and may take years to fully realize the tragic consequences. Neither is excusable!

Avoid Tomorrow's Tragedy

And the tragedy is that most parents do not realize that they, in spite of their outward demonstrations of love to their children, are dooming both them and their children to health problems affecting body, soul and spirit because of their lack of understanding and real concern on becoming selective!

In the book, *Live Longer Now*, the authors write:

> When good has been changed so that it no longer nourishes your body or becomes dangerous to your health, we call it garbage. . . .
>
> Much of what is being sold as food on your supermarket's shelves is not really food at all. It is garbage. It is garbage handsomely packaged and labeled as food, but it is garbage all the same.[1]

Supermarket bread, for the most part, is sugary, bleached bread devoid of nutrients. Even cereal weevils cannot maintain life on them!

Milling companies use chlorine, nitrogen or benzoyl peroxide as a bleaching agent to ar-

---

[1] Jon N. Leonard, J. L. Hofer, N. Pritikin, Live Longer Now (New York: Grosset & Dunlap), 1974, p. 117

rive at what the consumer wants: white bread. To fumigate the flour in storage, cyanide or chlorinated organic compounds may be used. Sulfur dioxide phosphates and lime can be used to refine the sugar put into the bread. The shortening is transformed to be financially productive for the milling company. Thus it is usually refined, bleached and deodorized and becomes a health-hazardous fat.

**Don't
Be Fooled
By TV
Commercials**

Television has warped our minds on guzzling soft drinks. The TV commercials picture vibrant youth prancing about, cycling down a forest path, skiing down a mountain, splashing through a stream and the subliminal seduction is saying: *"Hey, look how clean and wholesome all this activity is and our soft drink helps make it possible!"* But what are you actually drinking?

> carbonated sugar water
> phosphoric acid
> caffeine

Nutritionist Dr. Clive McKay dropped extracted human teeth in cola drinks. Within two days those teeth became very soft.

The phosphoric acid in soft drinks upsets the body's calcium-phosphorous balance and can also trigger an iron deficiency. A typical trait of high soft drink users is one of nervous tension, quickly changing moods and hyperactivity.

The caffeine stimulates the secretion of gastric acids and enzyme production. It can trigger nervousness, tremor, palpitation, insomnia, headaches and digestive disorders.

Gary and Steve Null, in their book, *The Complete Handbook of Nutrition*, write:

> *Certainly nothing was added to that egg you ate. An egg is an egg. But what about the hen that laid it? Do you know what chemicals went into her feed and sex hormones and antibiotics into her system?*
>
> *That tossed salad with dressing you had for lunch — were you aware of the sodium alginate (stabilizer), mono-isopropyl citrate (antioxidant to prevent fat deterioration), DDT and related compounds, phosphorus insecticide and week killers it contained?*
>
> *The juicy piece of roast beef you had for supper contained DDT and related compounds, methoxychlor, chlordane, heptachlor, toxaphene, lindane, benzene hexachloride, aldrin, dieldrin and other pesticides, particularly in the fatty parts, stilbestrol (artificial female sex hormone), aureomycin (antibiotic), mineral oil residue from wrapping paper. . . .*
>
> *What about that all-American apple pie — a fitting dessert of butylated hydroxyanisole (antioxidant in lard), chemical agents in flour and butter or margarine, sodium o-phenylphenate (preservative). . . .*[1]

I must admit it is becoming increasingly more

---

[1] Gary & Steve Null, The Complete Handbook of Nutrition (New York: Dell Publishing Co.), 1972, pp. 343, 344.

difficult to become selective in the foods that we eat. Regardless of how particular we may be, we are bound to eat some foods that contain additives. And although we do not smoke, we will inhale the smoke from those around us in public places. Our atmosphere has become dangerously polluted and we are prisoners within that environment. Therefore the air we breathe affects our health.

But, on the optimistic side, we can take some corrective measures to assure ourself and our loved ones of the most effective approach to what I call **"insular" nutrition** . . . that nutrition diet that seeks to insulate us from the ills of the world; that isolates us on an island of good health.

Ten Guidelines To Better Health

What are some of these SELECTIVE approaches?

A. <u>PLANT YOUR OWN GARDEN</u>

During the growing season, have your own garden. Turn part of your lawn into a garden. I did. Grow your own basic crops like endive, swiss chard, mustard greens, carrots, beets, eggplant, zucchini squash, parsley and mint. Such plants take little space but offer much in mineral-rich nutrition. You can also be sure they are not loaded with harmful sprays.

B. <u>EAT RAW FOODS</u>

As much as possible, make sure you eat a lot of raw vegetables daily. Strive to consume about 70% of your food intake daily in raw foods. Raw foods are still alive. They still contain active enzymes. And when they are digested, they can readily offer this live energy to your body.

**Provides
Roughage**

Raw foods also provide natural roughage and cellulose. These regulate the rate at which food is propelled along the bowel. Equally as important, they act as a broom to help remove the encrustations attached to the bowel wall. And cellulose is a natural detoxifier. It locks certain toxic substances in the bowel prohibiting them from becoming absorbed into your system.

**Preserves
Nutrients**

C. **STEAM instead of BOIL**

Naturally, you should not eat everything raw. But don't overcook food. Learn to steam your foods. Steaming breaks down the cellulose cell wall making the food easier to digest. Older persons initially cannot always tolerate a raw food diet. Here is where steaming can prove beneficial to them.

D. **USE SPROUTS**

**Provides
Energy**

You can have your own garden all winter long right on your kitchen window sill in just a few inches of space! And you can harvest your crop every 3-4 days. And you can have enough salad sprouts to feed a family of 4, twice a day! Sprouts are high on the list of quick-energy food. Sprouts jump in vitamin and mineral content almost overnight. They are a high power food . . . and their nutrition content remains very stable. They also freeze very successfully. When seeds begin to sprout, their vitamin content accelerates at a remarkable rate. The first shoots of soybeans (per 100 grams of seed) contain about 100 milligrams of vitamin C, but after 72 hours the content soars to approximately 700 milligrams, an increase of some 700 percent! This means that soybean sprouts contain almost 20 times the amount of vitamin C that is provided in a glass of orange juice. Similar comparisons can be made for most of the vitamins. Other sprouts are equally as beneficial. Alfalfa sprouts make delicious salads!

E. **DRINK SUFFICIENT LIQUIDS**

Propels Toxins

I personally believe that one should drink distilled water rather than tap water, well water or spring water. To determine daily water intake, I believe one should take their body weight (I'm 140 pounds); and divide it by two (140 ÷ 2 = 70). I should be drinking 70 ounces of distilled water daily. Develop a habit pattern in drinking water. I drink 4 ounces every half hour from about 9 AM to 6 PM. But I do not drink liquids during a meal, except to take my mineral supplements.

F. **EAT SALADS EVERY DAY**

Provides Minerals

When possible, eat two salads a day. By salad, I do not mean hearts of lettuce. This is extremely poor in nutritive values. I mean an assortment of greens like endive, spinach, sprouts, snap beans, kale, mustard greens or any dark, leafy vegetable plus cucumbers, parsley, mint and tomatoes.

**Protects
The Heart**

G. <u>RESTRICT YOUR MEAT INTAKE</u>
Americans eat far too much meat. Unless you are engaged in heavy labor, eat meat only three times a week at the most. I include chicken, turkey and fish as meat. Notice how much you improve as you lessen your intake of meat products. Of course, stay completely off of pork, shellfish and tuna fish. And eat meat well done, not rare. Also place the meat in brine overnight to drain out all the blood; or buy kosher meats. Do NOT eat meat at your evening meal. Meat requires at least six hours to digest. And partially digested protein can be toxic and may be involved in many physical and mental illnesses.

**Preserves
Assimilation**

H. <u>EAT FRUITS BY THEMSELVES</u>
Vary your meals by occasionally having an all-fruit lunch. Never mix other foods with the meal when fruit is your menu. Fruit is best eaten by itself. It is also best eaten before 2 PM. Most fruits are compatible one with the other. However, watermelon is best eaten alone with no other fruit.

Try a watermelon breakfast! You will be surprised how refreshingly it flushes toxins out of your body, giving you an exhilarating day! Eat fruits that are in season.

Partake Moderately

I. EASE INTO NUTS

Don't overdo nuts. Nuts are high stress foods. Many people with cancer, colitis, poor enzymes (due to a toxic liver or pancreas), diverticulitis, inflammed digestive tract or hemorrhoids will find that nuts further irritate their system. Avoid seed berries, such as strawberries, raspberries and blackberries. Almonds are an excellent nut. If you cannot tolerate nuts, try ground almonds or almond milk.

For Peak Power

J. LIVE FOODS FOR LIVE BODIES

As a general rule of thumb, remember, foods that spoil easily are the best foods to include in your diet. (Of course, eat them before they spoil.) Foods that spoil quickly are **live** foods. Foods that have a long shelf life are highly processed and embalmed foods that have little nutritive value and can be very toxic to your system. Get acquainted with yogurt and include it in your daily menu where possible. Buy yogurt made with skim milk and free of additives and sugars or fruits, which kill the friendly bacteria in yogurt. Yogurt also is an excellent calmative to eat just before retiring for the night. It will soothe your troubled nerves and at the same time fight the "unfriendly" bacteria in your colon.

These ten guidelines represent the basics of *The Getting Back to Nature Diet*. Follow them and you should notice an overall improvement in your general well-being. Also, remember, **eat only when you are hungry.** And never eat when upset or angry. And when you eat, leave the table without having that stuffed feeling. If you start to get sleepy, it is good indication you have eaten too much . . . and most likely you have foods that are "dead" foods.

Expect Withdrawal Symptoms

After eating the wrong foods for years, don't expect to make a change to healthy foods without suffering from withdrawal symptoms.

When you stop drinking such toxic stimulants as coffee, tea, chocolate or cocoa and soft drinks you will find yourself perhaps beset by nagging headaches and a general let-down feeling. This occurs because the toxins are being removed from the tissues and being transported through the blood stream to the eliminating organs.

And when the blood circulates through the brain during its many bodily rounds (before these toxic agents are eliminated), these irritants may cause headaches. These symptoms may vanish in several days. But the moment you cheat on your diet, they will come back like a raging river (perhaps even in greater intensity)!

You must give nature a chance to adjust in your system. You will notice improvements almost immediately but it may take 6 months to a year of a *Back to Nature Diet* before you are on a stable, vibrant life pattern. After all, if you have misused your body for years and fueled it with toxic fuel all these years, don't expect a complete reversal in one day. Ten or twenty years of misuse can be reversed in several months (6-12).

What To Expect

Actually in the first 10 days to 3 weeks of a diet reversal you may feel rather "pooped out" or under the weather. This is the crucial phase of your reversal pattern to healthy living. The body is once again becoming accustomed to good, nutritious food and is in a readjusting period as the toxins are being eliminated. When all the garbage is dumped out of the house and the new furniture is put in one will notice in about 3 weeks a gradual, steady improvement.

Cleansing The Bowel

The excess bile in the liver and gall bladder is sent to the intestines for elimination. The smelly, gassy, bowel masses are suddenly released and eliminated. Sludge moves out of the blood vessels. The toxic residues from food preservatives, aspirin, antihistamines, sleeping pills and prescription drugs are caught in the cleansing stream and slowly flushed out of your body.

The ashes that have been stagnating in your fuel system are suddenly being shoveled out in preparation for an effective firing system that will give you continued energy and strength.

It's like you have moved into a new house. You have a positive outlook on life . . . like the vibrancy and beauty of blossoming flowers in Spring.

Then something beautiful happens! The body starts to rebuild itself. It's like moving into a new house. All the old junk has been tossed aside. The old, frazzled wallpaper on the walls of your body are becoming transformed into live, vibrant skin and the wrinkles start to disappear. As the kidneys start functioning properly the bags under your eyes soon become less noticeable and then disappear. As you eat the right foods and your body begins to assimilate them properly, the putrefying bowel movements that occurred once a day or every other day are transformed into almost odorless bowel movements that occur twice a day.

A Wonderful Change

This, in part, is due to improved assimilation and increase of enzyme efficiency. At this stage your weight may increase even though you are eating less calories. But your weight will stablize at what is normal for your body frame.

The body's need for the usual amount of food will decrease. You will be able to maintain a steady weight and increase your energy with **less** food!

Visual Signs

Initially, upon switching to a *Back to Nature Diet,* you may notice skin rashes or eruptions on your face, ears or other parts of your body. You might wonder why this is occurring since you are eating better! Yet, it appears, because of these skin eruptions, that you are getting worse.

The reason is that the skin is getting more nutrients. Suddenly it is becoming alive and active. It is now throwing out more poisons

Nature's Way

more rapidly. This is because the body has more power. The toxins are being discarded through all your elimination organs. And skin is one of the eliminative organs. That is why the eruptions. You may even, temporarily, have colds or even fevers. This is all part of nature's way of getting rid of poisons that have long built up in your body. When nature does a housecleaning job, it does a thorough one. No nook or cranny is left undone . . . nor is anything swept under the rug! Most nutritionists recommend you let nature act without interference, without trying to stop these symptoms with drugs or massive doses of vitamins. These symptoms are part of the remedial process.

You may even experience a short interval of bowel sluggishness, occasional diarrhea, irritability or even frequent urination. These are tolerable conditions and will pass on as the body becomes readjusted to the *Back to Nature Diet*. It is always well to check with your doctor for guidance and consultation when you switch diets.

People view nature as they do food. To some people a tree is something so incredibly beautiful that it brings tears to their eyes. To others it is just a green thing that stands in the way of a shopping plaza.

Perhaps that is why wholesome raw vegetables are often treated as a "necessary" side dish—pushed aside for a hamburger and chocolate cake.

A group of visitors at a summer resort watched the sunset from the gallery of a hotel.

One man lingered till the last glow of the sun faded. One guest, more observant than the rest, commented: *"You certainly enjoyed that sunset, Mr. B. Are you an artist?"*

"No, madam," Mr. B. replied, *"I'm a plumber, but for five years I was blind."*

How many years have you been blind to supplying your body with the nutritious fuel it requires? Once you get back to nature in your total living pattern, you, too, will relish the vibrant warmth of the sun!

19

BE BALANCED

I once met a woman who looked like a carrot. Her face had the orange hue of a carrot. She explained to me that she had cancer and had heard that carrots were good for her. So for quite a long time she was subsisting solely on carrot juice.

She died a short time later!

There is no doubt that carrots are one of the most perfect foods. And carrot juice is extremely beneficial to one's health. But God also gave us other vegetables and fruits to fuel our body. I drink a carrot juice combination every day. But I include in it a pear, celery, and one-half a lemon as well as carrots and sometimes beet tops. Like many people, this lady did not follow a balanced diet.

Avoid Food Fads

We are bombarded constantly with all sorts of food fads; the grapefruit diet, the water diet, the *"eat-all-you-want and have a martini"* diet, the vinegar and apple cider diet, the high protein diet, the low protein diet, the save-your-life diet. And some people eat any kind of junk food because they are on the *"lose-your-life"* diet. Then, too, there are many doctors who subscribe to the *"pill for every ill"* diet and *"if it doesn't function, cut it out"* diet.

God has created our bodies with specific checks and balances. Dr. L. E. Maxwell, who for some 50 years, was President of Prairie Bible Institute in Three Hills, Alberta, Canada, has come up with a good guideline for living. Prairie Bible Institute does not offer the world's luxuries in living. Located in the middle of the prairies, the school is dedicated to training disciplined Christian soldiers for the battlefield of world missions. Six days a week the young men and women sit in separate sections both in the classroom and in the dining room. The reason: so they can devote their energies and thoughts to the training before them. Although many upon reading this may think this approach is old-fashioned, it works!

A Wise Observation

But the point I want to make is this. In the rigorous training of these young men and women, Dr. Maxwell has observed through the years that it is very easy for an individual to get off on a tangent. Some students may place too much emphasis and time on studying to the exclusion of recreation or fellowship. While, on the other hand, some may place too much time on fellowship without proper time on studies.

Then, too, because of the spiritual atmosphere of the campus, some may become "over spiritual" in that they become "no earthly good" and fail to function in society. They may devote so much time in prayer and praise that they fail to accomplish their studies or their work assignments. In off-hour jobs, they may spend time trying to convert a fellow employee when they should be giving their employer his full measure of time.

Everyone on the Prairie Bible Institute campus knows **MAXWELL 1:1** (as they call it). Those familiar with the Bible know that locations in the Bible are referred to first, by the book of the Bible, then the chapter and then the verse . . . such as Genesis 10:12. Well, Dr. L. E. Maxwell, through the years has suggested students and staff observe **MAXWELL 1:1** which is:

BE BALANCED

Achieving Perfect Harmony

Being balanced implies arriving at a mental and emotional stability. Body, soul and spirit must be balanced in perfect harmony if one expects to maintain good health or regain his or her health.

Envision a seesaw. You are sitting on one end. Your life style is placed on the other end. Is there an overemphasis in your lifestyle on food? Do you eat to live or do you live to eat? If you live to eat, soon the seesaw becomes unbalanced and so does your figure!

Is there an overemphasis on your own recreational pleasures and not sufficient emphasis on family fellowship? Your marriage may suffer.

Is there an overemphasis on work and not sufficient emphasis on getting acquainted with your children? Are you devoting a great deal of time to outside activities and not spending sufficient time at home? Are you devoting too much time to studying and not enough time to practical application of what you are learning? You may suffer a nervous breakdown.

Relax!

Do you know how to relax? Or are you constantly wound up, and never able to sit still? You are unbalanced.

BE BALANCED!

When the twelve disciples heard of the untimely death of John the Baptist, it was their task to take his body and bury it in a tomb. No doubt with great anxiety and sorrow they told Jesus of this tragic experience. And Jesus said to them:

> Come away by yourselves
> to a lonely place
> and rest a while.
>
> (Mark 6:31 ASV)

How important it is to get apart from the din of the world and reflect and refuel. Up until a few weeks ago I was going from morning to night trying to handle what appeared to be "a thousand and one details" and I never seemed to get all that I wanted to get accomplished by day's end.

Chewing Celery

By the evening I would sometimes be chewing two or three stalks of celery to calm me down. I would be so tense that by just flipping one of my strings you could probably play The Star Spangled Banner all the way through!

Our daughter, Diane, is now at Prairie Bible Institute. But I remembered when she was

I begin my day by reading a chapter in the Bible and praying. The Bible says: "Be anxious for nothing, but in everything by prayer and supplication with thanksgiving let your requests be made known to God" (Philippians 4:6). Following these guidelines, I find complete peace of mind throughout the entire day.

home she would sit in a rocking chair in her room reading the Bible in the early morning.

I Found The Secret

It was then I found the secret! A few weeks ago I started the same thing. After getting dressed, I sit in her rocking chair, and read systematically the Word of God. Right now I am in the book of Psalms. I not only read one Psalm a day but keep a notebook handy to record all the promises and lessons in living in that chapter.

May I make a confession? I am no longer tense by the end of the day. And even though I take 15 minutes out for this reflection, I find I am able to accomplish **far more** than I did before. It seems incredible! I also have peace of mind and am able to think far more clearly. And I have found a new joy!

Someone has said that

> Prayer is the key of the morning
> and
> the bolt of the night.

After reading the Word, I kneel and ask God to guide my footsteps during the day. It becomes more difficult to stumble if you are on your knees!

I do not mean to infer that when you pray, everything is going to work out to your desires. You may still make some stupid mistakes. But when we pray for rain we must be willing to put up with some mud.

Now what would you think of a person if he spent all his time praying and no time fulfilling his daily responsibilities? He certainly would not be balanced.

**Who
Is
"Policy"**

I find that many people are <u>inflexible.</u> They are not able to bend. One of my pet peeves is the individual who tells me: *"Sorry, that is company <u>policy</u>."* The world seems to run on either *"company policy"* or *"government policy."* It is as though policy is created by some machine made with nuts and bolts. Generally such "policies" are ridiculous, in my opinion. I usually say to the individual:

*Now, think for yourself a minute.
Who is "policy?" Is he your next door neighbor?
Is he a cherished friend?
Everywhere I go I hear people talking about "policy."
He must be pretty influential and do a lot of travelling.*

Everywhere I go I find people bowing and scraping before him. Why, I have met "policy" in Vietnam, in Japan, in Jordan, in Israel, in Lebanon, and in Canada. I have even met "policy" in the United States in manufacturing plants, in department stores, and even in hospitals. (Policy wasn't sick, he was just visiting, apparently.)

*Now, who is "policy?"
(Then I lower the boom)
Don't you realize that "policy" is
        <u>made by people!</u>
And people change. Therefore "policy" can change.*

However, I am sad to report, in spite of all my protests and reasonings, very rarely is "policy" moved. We are a world of people who are, for the most part, very inflexible.

Yet, one prime example that touched me about how fragile our lives are . . . was the day that President Kennedy died. Within a few hours the movers were moving his Presidential chair and furniture out of the oval office. office. The world gets so uptight on "policy" and protocol. But their importance is soon lost down the corridors of time. Do not be inflexible! **BEND!**

Be Flexible

Good health encompasses your entire life style. How long do you think an airplane wing would withstand the turbulence if it failed to bend! How long would a skyscraper remain standing if it failed to bend and sway with the wind!

BE BALANCED. BE FLEXIBLE. Two good rules for healthy living . . . a living that gets back to the back to nature diet. Don't eat the same thing for breakfast every day . . . or for lunch or supper. Vary your diet. But make sure that diet has *"live foods for live bodies."*

Enjoy every minute of your life. But be careful what you place into your body, into your mind and into your soul. Make sure all three feed on wholesome ingredients and not the garbage of the world.

It was Mark Twain who remarked:

> *I don't know of a single foreign prod-
> uct that enters this country untaxed,
> except the answer to prayer.*

BE BALANCED! I'm going to practice what I preach. I have spent the last two hours typing this chapter. Now, I am going to stop, go out to the garden, get some lettuce, parsley, mint and beets and have a light lunch. I could write 5 chapters a day. But I would be unbalanced in my time. And, in my opinion, my writing would suffer. What about your life? Have you learned the secret of being flexible. And are you BALANCED?

20

HOW TO DISCOVER LIFE'S TRUE VALUES

Our home is quieter now.

My wife and I are in our early 50's. Of our five children, only **Duane** is presently living at home.

Three of our children are some 3000 miles away from home.

> **Doreen**
> (whose photo appears on the front cover of this book)
> is married and living in Washington state.

> **Diane and Dawn**
> are attending Prairie Bible Institute and Prairie High School in Three Hills, Alberta, Canada.

Dennis, our oldest, is married and living nearby. It is hard to believe that he is already 30. Somehow it gives us a perspective we never realized before.

Honey and Lemon

We remember the school play our daughter, Doreen, took part in. She was just 13. The play was *The Mikado.* Doreen was Yum Yum and she had a leading singing role. That afternoon she came home hoarse. She could not talk.

Normally, it's a time when mothers throw up their hands in excited concern or utter resignation.

The year was 1967. Our daughter, Doreen, was to play Yum Yum in the play, The Mikado, at Lower Moreland school in Huntingdon Valley. That afternoon she came home hoarse. And my wife remembered an old-fashioned remedy her mother had taught her . . . honey and lemon. That night Doreen sang beautifully!

But my wife remembered an old-fashioned remedy her mother had taught her:

honey and lemon

That night Doreen sang beautifully!

As I write this . . . it is 10 years since that memorable evening. My wife quietly catches up on her sewing and I am just reflecting on life and the sweet memories our children gave us.

A Greater Responsibility

But the past is just a stepping stone to the future. And as parents, and now grand-parents, we have even greater responsibilities. For our children and their children need us even more.

Part of the love we share is helping them take care of their health. It is a treasure worth guarding.

The Bible tells us:

Thy hands made me and fashioned me.
Thou didst form my inward parts;
Thou didst weave me in my
         mother's womb.
I will give thanks to Thee,
     for I am fearfully
     and wonderfully made.
     (Psalm 119:73a; 139:13b-14a NAS)

We are also reminded:

Do you not know
that your body
is a temple of the Holy Spirit . . .
therefore glorify God in your body.
     (1 Corinthians 6:19 and 20b NAS)

Then we are warned:

> Do you not know
> that you are a temple of God . . .
> If any man destroys
> the temple of God,
> God will destroy him,
> for the temple of God is holy,
> and that is what you are.
>
> (1 Corinthians 3:16-17 NAS)

It was Apostle John who wrote:

> Beloved, I pray that in all respects
> you may prosper
> and be in good health . . .
>
> (3 John 2 NAS)

A Question of Values

I can never understand how people take better care of their steam irons and their automobile than they do of their own bodies. Then, when their body starts to rebel, they run to their doctor looking for the miracle drug or new sophisticated surgery that can give them a new lease on life. Actually, they are just borrowing time and sooner or later the abuse done to the body will claim its toll.

I am no longer surprised at the contradictions in life.

HEW (Health, Education and Welfare) lists some 16,500 chemicals that are toxic of which 1500 are suspected of causing cancer and 250 of producing birth defects. And hundreds of new chemicals are introduced commercially each year. Over 25 products contain the dangerous pesticide called DBCP. More than 25 million pounds of this are pro-

duced each year. Such a product causes ste-
rility and is believed to be a cancer-causitive
agent yet it is regularly applied on fruits and
vegetables and you and I, unknowingly, eat
it! And yet no warning signs appear in our
supermarkets.

But the Federal Government posted signs in
Federal buildings stating: LAETRILE IS
WORTHLESS. And, it may be. Time will tell.
But so are cigarettes. So is liquor. So are many
television programs. So are many magazines.
So are soft drinks.

**The
Tragedy**

Americans spend over $65 per person on soft
drinks every year and only $14 on fruit and
vegetable juices!

Cola companies remind us that this is the
"in" generation. Do your thing. Be a part of
the crowd. Enjoy life. Do it your way. And
millions of people do!

After they have matured from the Cola crowd
they realize that "they only go around once"
so they start living it up with beer. They look
for the "light and lively" beer that can give
them new thrills.

And, of course, every knowledgeable teenager must mature by learning how to drink
liquor intelligently. Many times his parents
teach him how.

Cigarettes are a way of life in high schools
today. Special "smoke breaks" are given and
sometimes designated smoking rooms are
supplied.

To further feed the body, school children are
given substantial lunches that usually consist

of spaghetti, pizza, cola, french fries, cookies and cake.

They can't wait to get out of school to cruise around in their car which they have pampered with the highest grade oil, the best spark plugs, wire wheels and expensive chrome trim and an engine so clean you could eat your lunch off of it! They know they can't get away with cheating on the care of their car. Their body? Well, that's something different!

They allow their ears to be pounded by the blaring music of this generation and soon develop a premature deafness. It has often been said: "We tend to live on the level of the music we listen to."

The Harvest

We are now reaping the harvest of such misuse of the human body. Now <u>even children</u> are suffering from ulcers. Ulcers used to be a middle-age syndrome. Children are already on tranquilizers. Catastrophic diseases are reaping a high toll on the teenager.

Suicides and crime among teenagers has risen dramatically. In the late 60's and early 70's we were faced with the widespread use of illegal drugs. Now, teenagers are filling their bodies with legal drugs and legal alcoholic beverages.

Permissiveness is on every hand. There is a lack of discipline; a turning away from the principles based on the Bible. These are all responsible for the pollution of body, soul and spirit.

We are sick!

It is time to rediscover life's true values.

This may be considered old-fashioned.

It is unfortunate that today so many people are demanding something for nothing. It is even more unfortunate that they are getting it. If the next generation grows up with the same values of many people living today, you can look for chaos among the human race.

In man's race for wealth, he often sacrifices his health. Then when he reaches the pinnacle of worldly acclaim and loses his health . . . he suddenly discovers health is a commodity money cannot buy!

Weigh Your Priorities

The Arab was telling of the time he had lost his way in the desert. Just as he was about to abandon hope and let his hunger overcome him in death, he found a bag of pearls. *"I shall never forget,"* he said, *"the relish and delight I felt supposing the contents of the bag to be dried wheat, nor the bitterness and despair I suffered in discovering that the bag contained nothing but pearls."*

It was Roger Babson, the statistician, who was lunching with the President of Argentina when the President asked him:

> *Mr. Babson, I have been wondering why it is that South America with all its natural resources, its mines, its rivers and great waterfalls which rival Niagara, is so far behind America.*

Babson replied:
> *Well, Mr. President, what do you think is the reason?*

The President of Argentina was silent for a moment. Then he answered:

Above are listed **all** the material possessions you will be able to take with you when you die! **NONE!** Where are you devoting all your energy, your time and your money? Be honest in answering this question. Perhaps it is time to realign your priorities emphasizing those priorities that are beyond price and that are enduring.

I have come to this conclusion. South America was settled by the Spanish, who came to South America in search of gold. But North America was settled by the Pilgrim Fathers, who went there in search of God.

A tourist one day came upon a talented Navajo squaw. He requested that she weave him a rug with some of the religious symbols of America on it.

When she solemnly delivered it and got her pay, the tourist realized how others see us. Instead of a church steeple and a Bible or angel, she had woven the pictures of an automobile and a bottle of liquor!

When a man is born, people say, *"How is the mother?"* When he marries, they say, *"What a beautiful bride!"* And when he dies, they say, *"How much did he leave her?"*

**A Return
To
Yesterday's
Values**

Today we are afraid of simple words like goodness and mercy and kindness. We don't believe in the good old words because we don't believe in the good old values any more.

Have you ever stopped to ask yourself the question?

> *How much would you be worth if you lost all your money?*

A minister and a fighter pilot were playing golf. A jet plane flew over. *"How fast is he going?"* the minister asked.

"About 500 miles per hour," was the answer.

When a slower plane droned over, the airman said:

"That's one we used for rescue at sea. He's going only 150 miles per hour." Then, he added: *"Silly, isn't it? If you're going to kill somebody, you go 500 miles an hour. If you're just going to save a life, you slow down to 150 miles an hour!"*

How fast are you travelling through life? 500 miles an hour? Or 150 miles an hour? Are you living life to the hilt, seeking out every physical joy, climbing the financial ladder to reach the end of that elusive rainbow? Are you treating your body like a garbage dump and your possessions like Fort Knox?

Stop Right Now! Isn't it time you stopped . . . right now! Is it at all possible for you . . . **right this very minute** . . . right now . . . to drop **EVERYTHING** you are doing, DISMISS all matters of concern from your mind . . . and go **right now** to the quietest room in your home. Close the door. Sit in a comfortable chair. Place the Bible in your lap and slowly read some of the Psalms **FOR ONE SOLID HOUR** in quietness and without interruption!

Then after a few minutes of meditation in the Bible, take a notebook. Write down on one side all your material possessions; your home, your car, your furniture, your clothing.

On the other side write down all the possessions that money **cannot** buy; your health, your peace of mind, the harmony in your home, your spiritual values. Then take inventory.

Howard Hughes was the wealthiest man in the world. But he could not buy back one more minute of good health. Some have wondered just how much money Howard Hughes left when he died. <u>HE LEFT ALL OF IT!</u>

A Challenge That Can Change Your Life

The next two pages are BLANK. Isn't it time you took an inventory of your life . . . right now. Don't put it off till tomorrow. All things come to him who waits, except tomorrow!

Are you strong enough to determine that you will spend ONE COMPLETE HOUR alone with yourself in a quiet room, uninterrupted? Or are you physically, morally and spiritually weak? Right now, take the phone off the hook . . . go to your room with a Bible, a pencil and a pad (or use the next two pages) to DISCOVER YOURSELF. You may be surprised at what is revealed as you honestly take a tally of your life. You will immediately realize your weaknesses. And all of us have weaknesses.

But, once you realize these weaknesses, these misdirected goals . . . **then DO SOMETHING about it.**

Do it now. Then why not write me and let me know how you changed your life. (Salem Kirban, Kent Road, Huntingdon Valley, Penna. 19006 U.S.A.)

DISCOVERING LIFE'S TRUE VALUES

MY MATERIAL POSSESSIONS

(List items of material value here such as Clothes - $450, Automobile - $3500, Camera - $70, Furniture - $5200, House, Hobby and Sport equipment, Bank Account, Insurance, etc.)

On this side, list items of material value you *now* possess and estimate their dollar value.

On this side, list items of material value you are striving or desire to possess (such as: New Job, Promotion, New Car, Television Set, Golf Clubs, Refrigerator, Bedroom Set, Rugs, etc.)

ITEMS I NOW POSSESS		ITEMS I DESIRE TO POSSESS	
ITEM	$ VALUE	ITEM	$ VALUE
1. House	$	1.	$
2. Automobile		2.	
3. Furniture		3.	
4. Clothing		4.	
5. Television		5.	
6. Savings Account		6.	
7. Investments		7.	
8.		8.	
9.		9.	
10.		10.	
11.		11.	
12.		12.	
13.		13.	
14.		14.	
15.		15.	
TOTAL VALUE	$	TOTAL VALUE	$

Place here Total of **BOTH** Columns $

Do not be afraid when a man becomes rich, When the glory of his house is increased; For when he dies he will carry nothing away; His glory will not descend after him. (Psalm 49:16-17)

DISCOVERING LIFE'S TRUE VALUES

POSSESSIONS
MONEY CANNOT BUY

On a Marking Scale of 1 to 3, grade your estimate of achievement in accumulating possessions that money cannot buy.

Place a **1** under Sale of Achievement if you have **not** achieved this goal. Place a **2** under Scale of Achievement if you **occasionally** achieve this goal. Place a **3** under Scale of Achievement if you have **successfully** achieved this goal.

POSSESSIONS MONEY CANNOT BUY	Scale of Achievement
1. Eternal Life, (John 3:16; Romans 6:23; 10:9)	
2. Harmony in Your Home	
3. A Fulfilled Happy Marriage	
4. Love and Respect from your Children	
5. Family Devotions	
6. Personal Morning and Evening Devotions	
7. Attend Church Faithfully	
8. The ability to say: "I'm sorry."	
9. The ability to say: "I made a mistake."	
10. Peace of Mind	
11. Abundant Health	
12. Freedom from Fear	
13. Freedom from Worry	
14. Exhibit Joy through Trials	
15. A Thankful Happy Heart	

Total Scale of Achievement ➤

40 - 45	You have discovered Life's true values!
35 - 39	You are making progress. Check your weak points and strive to bring them up to Scale 3 level.
25 - 34	You need to realign your priorities in life. Are you seeking the best of both worlds? You can't serve two masters! Honestly appraise your life's direction and plan to change your priorities.
Under 25	You should very seriously reexamine your life and your goals in light of eternal values. Your priorities are misappropriated. Make major changes now while you still have time.

The Getting Back to Nature Diet is an overall diet not only of eating the proper foods for a healthy body but also rediscovering life's true values. It took me a long time to rediscover life's true values. I found the secret some 3000 miles away from home on the prairies of Canada unhindered by signs and shopping centers and the mad rush of civilization. **You can do it right in your own home.**

Make The Right Decision

If you just put this book aside and don't invest in this HOUR OF POWER, your life will soon burn out, for in not discovering life's true values, you will be short circuiting your time on this earth, and no penny in the fuse box of life is going to give you happiness nor peace!

As it was the Apostle John's, it is also my prayer that in all respects . . .

> You may prosper
> and be in good health!

Throughout my lecture tours, I have many times told the story about East Berlin and West Berlin. East Berlin is under Communist control. West Berlin is free.

The people of East Berlin loaded a truck with garbage and dumped it on the West Berlin side.

The people of West Berlin could have done the same thing. But they instead loaded a truck with butter, eggs, canned goods and honey and neatly stacked it on the East Berlin side, with this sign:

EACH GIVES WHAT HE HAS

SEED THOUGHTS FROM SALEM
(Valuable Cooking Hints)

<u>Bread</u>
The woman who used to bake a dozen loaves of bread a week, now has a granddaughter who complains if she has to toast half a dozen slices. Don't loaf away your time and then depend on the Lord for your daily bread; He isn't running a bakery.

1. <u>Enrich your bread when baking</u>
   For each
       1/4 cup of white flour
   substitute
       2 tablespoons of raw wheat germ
       2 tablespoons of soy flour
   This is the equivalent of 1/4 cup.

2. <u>Yeast</u>
   Yeast is very particular about how it is treated. It will give up and stop working if it is **overheated**, or if it is **chilled**. Dissolve yeast in lukewarm liquid.

   Yeast loves honey. If you add 1 teaspoon of honey to the dissolving yeast, it will work faster.

3. <u>Rising bread</u>
   It took me 20 loaves to find out the secret of how to make bread rise. I place it in the oven, without heat, and cover it with a damp cloth. I place a pan of water on the bottom oven shelf. This provides the humidity. (If your oven is too cold, heat it briefly, then turn it off; then place dough in oven.)

4. <u>Whole Grain breads</u>
   It is best to oil your bread pan **liberally** when using whole grain breads. This prevents sticking. If you are not going to eat it right away, put it in the freezer, rather than the frige. It will dry out too quickly in the frige.

5. <u>Yeasty bread</u>
   Ugh! I baked some bread that turned out yeasty or "sour." Thought I had used too much yeast. Not so, however! The problem usually is that you either did not keep the dough warm enough or it was allowed to rise too much. Tough. Try again!

SEED THOUGHTS FROM SALEM
(Valuable Cooking Hints)

Soups

I don't know about you, but I love to make soups. Somehow it sparks the creative "genius" in me. I must admit I've had some failures. But it was good experience. Experience is like drawing without an eraser. Experience is the only teacher that gives the test first and the lesson later. And now my soups are most delicious!

1. Thickening agents
   Blend together rice and soy flours.

2. Preparation
   Make your soup stock a day in advance. Put in frige overnight. The fat will rise to the top. Then, the next day, whammo! skim the fat off. The more you skim off **it** the less you will have to skim off **you**!

3. Vegetables
   Sauté them first in oil to seal in the flavor and keep them firm. Excellent oils are corn, soybean or olive.

4. Meat
   Never boil meat in soup. This toughens the meat. Put meat in when soup is just simmering. What a difference!

GOLDEN NUGGETS OF COOKING INFORMATION

Have you ever been frustrated? Reminds me of the woman making arrangements with an artist to sit for her portrait. She requested: *"Although I have only a few items of jewelry, nevertheless, I want this painting to show me wearing diamond rings and earrings, an emerald brooch, and a multistrand necklace of pearls that look like they are priceless."*

"I can do this all right," said the artist, *"But you and I know that you don't own such jewelry and live modestly. Tell me, why do you want me to paint a picture showing such costly jewels?"*

"You see, if I die first," said the woman, *"and my husband marries again, I want that second wife to go out of her mind trying to find where I hid the jewels."*

Seriously though, it is frustrating when you decide to cook or bake and discover you need some vital information but just *"don't know where to put my hands on it."* Perhaps these Golden Nuggets of cooking information may prove useful.

Honey

Those who are nutrition minded prefer to substitute honey for sugar. You must remember that honey has greater sweetening power, however. Therefore you substitute 1 cup honey for **each** 1 1/4 cups sugar. Also be sure to **reduce** the liquid in the recipe by 1/4 cup. It is best to **add** a pinch of baking soda as well so the end product does not turn out too brown. This also neutralizes the acidity in the honey.

Liquid Measure Volume Equivalents

1 teaspoon	=	1/3 tablespoon
1 tablespoon	=	3 teaspoons
2 tablespoons	=	1 fluid ounce
4 tablespoons	=	2 ounces or 1/4 cup
8 tablespoons	=	4 ounces or 1/2 cup
1/4 cup	=	4 tablespoons or 2 fluid ounces
1/3 cup	=	5 1/3 tablespoons
1/2 cup	=	8 tablespoons or 4 fluid ounces or 1/4 pint
1 cup	=	16 tablespoons or 8 fluid ounces or 1/2 pint
2 cups	=	1 pint or 16 fluid ounces
1 pint liquid	=	16 fluid ounces or 2 cups
1 quart, liquid	=	2 pints or 4 cups (32 fluid ounces)
1 gallon, liquid	=	4 quarts (128 fluid ounces) and that's a lot of soup!

Sugar Weights

1 cup confectioners' weighs	4½ ounces
1 cup granulated weighs	8 ounces
1 cup brown sugar weighs	6 ounces
1 cup corn syrup weighs	12 ounces
1 cup molasses or honey weighs	12 ounces

Let's Not Glory in the Celsius

It seems like the rest of the world is trying to change Americans into thinking in metric measures. And now weather temperatures are not given in simply Fahrenheit but also a measuring unit called Celsius or centigrade. Fahrenheit was a German physicist and Celsius was a Swedish astronomer. And it looks like Anders Celsius saw his fortune in the stars for Celsius is gaining in popularity. But, personally, I would vote for Gabrial Daniel Fahrenheit. Anyone with  a Bible name like that (Gabrial and Daniel) can't be all that bad! Now, doesn't that golden bit of information add more sunshine to your life today!

Anyway, here are the approximate temperature conversions should Mr. Anders Celsius have his way.

	Fahrenheit	Celsius (centigrade)
Freezer	0°	-17°
Water freezes	32°	0°
Water simmers	115°	46°
Water boils	212°	100°
Very low oven	250°	121°
Low oven	300°	149°
Moderate oven	350°	177°
Hot oven	400°	204°
Very hot oven	450°	232°

For those of you who are mathematically inclined: to convert Fahrenheit into Celsius (centigrade) . . . subtract 32, multiply by 5 and then divide by 9. Don't ask me to explain it. I flunked Algebra. In fact they said I should be a chiropodist. Why? Because I was always at the foot of the class! Oh for the days when life was simple and uncomplicated. Science is wonderful. For years uranium cost only a few dollars a ton until scientists discovered you could kill people with it.

EQUIVALENTS and SUBSTITUTIONS

Did you ever wonder how many cups in a 1 lb. bag of raisins? The answer is NONE! They generally don't insert cups in bags of raisins these days. Now in the good old days you could get an Orphan Annie secret whistle in a box of cereal! Anyway, it is good to know some basic equivalents when you are energetic and want to try something new.

	Unit	Equivalent
Almonds		
Unblanched, whole	6 oz.	1 cup
Unblanched, ground	1 lb.	2 2/3 cups
Unblanched, slivered	1 lb.	5 2/3 cups
Apples		
Whole	1 lb. unpared	3 cups pared, sliced
Whole for drying	10 applies	1 lb. dried
Apricots, dried	1 lb.	3 1/4 cups
Arrowroot powder (as thickener)	1 1/2 teaspoons	1 tablespoon flour
	2 teaspoons	1 tablespoon cornstarch
Baking powder		
rising equivalent	1 teaspoon	1/4 teaspoon baking soda plus 1/2 cup buttermilk or yogurt
	1 teaspoon	1/4 teaspoon baking soda plus 1/4 to 1/2 cup molasses
Bananas	3 to 4 med. size	1 3/4 cups mashed
Bay leaf	1/4 teaspoon	1 whole bay leaf

	Unit	Equivalent
Bread crumbs, dry	1/4 cup	1 slice bread
Butter		
1 stick	4 ounces	8 tablespoons or 1/2 cup
4 sticks	1 lb.	2 cups
Buttermilk	1 cup	1 cup yogurt
Cabbage	1 head (1 lb.)	4 1/2 cups shredded
Carob powder	3 tablespoons plus 2 tablespoons of water	1 oz. chocolate
Carrots	1 lb.	3 cups shredded (2 1/2 cups diced)
Cheese, cream	3 ounces	6 tablespoons
Chocolate, unsweetened	1 ounce	3 tablespoons carob powder plus 2 tablespoons of water
Cracker crumbs	3/4 cup	1 cup bread crumbs
Eggs		
large 2 ounce	5	1 cup approx.
medium	6	1 cup approx.
small	7	1 cup approx.
Flour, all-purpose		
white	4 cups	3 1/2 cups cracked wheat
white	1 cup	1 cup cornmeal
		or
		1 1/4 cups rye flour
		or
		7/8 cup gluten flour
		or
		1/2 cup whole wheat flour plus 1/2 cup flour
		or
		1/2 cup bran plus 1/2 cup flour
		or
		1/3 cup soybean plus 2/3 cup flour

	Unit	Equivalent
Garlic	1 clove	1/8 teaspoon powder
Horseradish	1 tablespoon fresh, grated	2 tablespoons bottled
Lemon	1	2 tablespoons juice approx.
	1 teaspoon grated rind	1/2 teaspoon lemon extract
Lentils	1 lb. (2 1/4 cups)	5 cups cooked
Milk, whole	1 quart	1 quart skim milk plus 3 tablespoons cream
Milk, skim	1 cup	1/3 cup instant nonfat dry milk plus 3/4 cup water
Oatmeal	1 cup uncooked	1 3/4 cups cooked
Raisins, seedless	1 lb.	2 3/4 cups
Rice, precooked	2 cups	2 2/3 cups cooked
Rice, regular	2 cups uncooked	6 cups cooked
Rolled oats	1 lb.	8 cups cooked
Saccharin	1/4 grain	1 teaspoon sugar
Tapioca	2 tablespoons quick-cooking	4 tablespoons pearl, soaked
Wheat Germ	12 ounces	3 cups
Yeast, compressed	1 cake (3/5 ounce)	1 package active dry yeast
Yeast, active dry	1 package	1 tablespoon
Yogurt	1 cup	1 cup buttermilk

I hope these equivalent and substitution tables will help you. The more you can substitute live, nutritional foods for highly processed or sugary ingredients the better off you will be. A wise man once said, "*Tell me what you eat, and I'll tell you what you are.*"

KEY TO READING FOOD CHARTS

The Food Charts on the following pages are divided into 11 categories:

1. Meat and Poultry
2. Fish
3. Eggs
4. Milk and Dairy Products
5. Vegetables and Vegetable Products
6. Dry Beans, Peas and Nuts
7. Fruit and Fruit Products
8. Cereal, Grains and Grain Products
9. Fats and Oils
10. Sugars, Sweets and Syrups
11. Food Juices, Beverages

Bold Face Numerals
For each food listed, the highest mineral or vitamin content is printed in a bold face. As an example, in Chart 1 of Meat and Poultry . . . under Beef . . . the Chuck, boneless is highest in Potassium. Therefore the **354** milligrams is printed in **bold face type**.

Asterisks (*)
Some foods are preceded by an asterisk (*). These are foods which should **not** be included in your diet. There are unclean foods. But more important, they release their energy too quickly for the body to make use of them. They digest so fast that you cannot use the proteins, which turn into urea and dump into the bloodstream so fast that the kidneys cannot eliminate them. A urea build-up in the body ensues and excessive urea leads to many health problems.

High Stress Foods
The Food Charts indicate which foods are High Stress Foods. High Stress Foods should **not** be a major part of your food intake. You will find that eating too many High Stress Foods robs your body of energy. Plan your meals around **low stress** foods for better health.

Low Stress Foods
Low Stress Foods digest easily and quickly. They leave very little residue for the liver to detoxify. And, they do not cause toxic build-up in the colon or vascular system. Because Low Stress Foods are more easily digested, the (a) offer their energy more readily to the body and (b) conserve energy that would otherwise be used in trying to digest High Stress Foods. Therefore, this energy can be used to increase energy reserves and increase endurance.

1. MEAT and POULTRY

Food	Food Energy Calories	Protein	Fat	Carbo-hydrates	Cal-cium	Phos-phorus	Iron	So-dium	Potas-sium	Magne-sium	Manga-nese	Zinc	Vitamin A	Vitamin C
HIGH STRESS														
Beef														
Chuck, boneless	257	18.7	19.6	0	11	168.2	2.8	64.9	**354**	18.5			39.6	
Corned hash, canned	199	8.9	14.6	8.09	26.1	69.6	1.2	**540**	200	21.2			tr	
Ground	263	25.6	17.0	0	7.1	220	3.9	47	**449.2**	4.6			30	6
Heart	108	16.9	3.7	0.7	9	**203**	4.6	90	160					
Kidney	141	15.0	8.1	0.9	9	221	7.9	**245**	231	18			1150	13
Liver, beef	136	19.7	3.2	6.0	7	**358**	6.6	86	325	21			**43,900**	31
Liver, calf	141	19.0	4.9	4.0	6	343	10.6	131	436	24			**22,500**	36
Lungs	96	17.6	2.3	0		**216**								
Porterhouse	242	25.4	14.7	0	11	183	3.8	52	**398**	20				
Potpie	195	7.3	11.2	16.3	6.2	48	1.5	**366**	93				617.2	
Ribs, lean	171	26.8	6.3	0	9.8	205	3.4	41.5	412.4	22.0				
Round, bottom	238	35.5	9.5	0	12.3	228	5.3	44.7	**484**	24.6				
Rump	235	32	10.9	0	8.8	197.5	4.8	53.8	**386.2**	20.0				
Sweetbreads	184	15.2	13.2	0	10	**400**	1.2	96	360				17	44
T-bone, broiled	247	25.3	15.5	0	10.5	181.1	3.8	51.6	**398**	20.0				
Tongue	208	16.4	15.1	0.4	8.1	182.3	2.1	73.3	**197.4**	16				
Brains	125	10.4	8.6	0.8	10.6	**311.8**	2.4	124.7	218.8					17.6

Food	Basic Food Elements						MINERALS (Milligrams)						VITAMINS	
	Food Energy Calories	Protein	Fat	Carbo-hydrates	Cal-cium	Phos-phorus	Iron	So-dium	Potas-sium	Magne-sium	Manga-nese	Zinc	Vitamin A	Vitamin C
Chicken														
Boned, canned	178	20.4	10.0	0.2	14	149	1.8		138					
Breast, fryer	104	23.3	0.5	0	14	212	1.1	90	370					
Broiler	151	20.2	7.2	0	14	200	1.5	78	320					
Gizzard	113	20.1	2.7	0.7	9.9	105.1	2.9	65.1	240.4					
Leg, fryer	112	20.5	2.7	0	15	188	1.8	79	325					
Liver	141	22.1	4.0	2.6	16	240	7.4	76.6	188				32,200	20
Potpie	198	8.3	10.4	17.4	16.4	101.7	1.0	411	153				123.3	5.2
Roaster	200	20.2	2.6	0	14	200	1.5	78	320					
Lamb														
Blade chop, lean	34	22.8	27	0	10	179	1.5	70	290	22				
Leg, lean, roasted	192	28.6	7.7	0	12	237	2.2	70	290	22				
Liver	261	32.3	12.4	2.8	16	572	17.9	85	331				74,500	36
Loin, lean	188	28.2	7.8	0	12	219	2.0	70	290	20				
***Pork**														
Blade, lean	245	27.6	14.1	0	12	287	3.5	65	390	20				
Lion chop, broiled	418	23.5	35.2	0	10	256	3.2	65	390	22				
Picnic ham	323	22.4	25.2	0	10	182	2.9		25					
Spare ribs	440	28.8	38.9	0	9	121	2.6	65	390					
Turkey														
Roasted	200	30.9	7.6	0	30	400	5.1	129.5	367	28			10	
Veal														
Cutlet	277	33.2	15.0	0	10	288	4.2	54	527	23				
Loin chop	421	22.7	35.9	0	6	187	2.9	44	314	16				
Sirloin	274	23.9	19.1	0	8	221	3.0	53	476	19				

Food	Basic Food Elements				MINERALS (Milligrams)								VITAMINS	
	Food Energy Calories	Protein	Fat	Carbo-hydrates	Cal-cium	Phos-phorus	Iron	So-dium	Potas-sium	Magne-sium	Manga-nese	Zinc	Vitamin A	Vitamin C
HIGH STRESS														
Anchovy, canned	175	19.2	10	trace	166.6	**208.2**								
Bass, striped	105	18.9	2.7	0										
Caviar, pressed, canned	320	34	17	5		**212**		22	18					
*Clams														
Hard, raw	80	11.1	0.9	5.9	69	151	7.5	205	**311**			1.5		
Soft, raw	82	14.0	1.9	1.3		183	3.4	36	235			1.5		
Clam chowder	30	0.9	1.0	4.1	17.5	21.5	0.4	**414**						
Cod	78	17.6	0.3	0	10	194	0.4	70	**382**	28				2
*Crab, steamed	93	17.3	1.9	0.5	43	**175**	0.8			34				2
*Fish cakes	172	14.7	8.0	9.3	—	—							**2170**	
Flounder	68	14.9	0.5	0	61	195	0.8	56	**366**	30			—	—
*Frog legs	73	16.4	0.3	0	18	**147**	1.5					0.7		
Halibut	100	20.9	1.2	0	13	211	0.7	54	**449**				440	
*Lobster														
Meat only	91	16.9	1.9	0.5	29.1	**183**	0.6							
Newburg	194	18.5	10.6	5.1	87	192	0.9	**229**	171					
*Oysters														
Eastern, raw	66	8.4	1.8	3.4	94	**143**	5.5	73	121	32		74.7	310	30
Western, raw	91	10.6	2.2	6.4	85	**153**	7.2							

| Food | Basic Food Elements | | | | MINERALS (Milligrams) | | | | | | | | VITAMINS | |
	Food Energy Calories	Protein	Fat	Carbohydrates	Calcium	Phosphorus	Iron	Sodium	Potassium	Magnesium	Manganese	Zinc	Vitamin A	Vitamin C
Salmon														
Atlantic	217	22.5	13.4	0	79	**186**	0.9							9
Chinook	222	19.1	15.6	0		301		45	**399**				310	
Pink	119	20.0	3.7	0				64	**306**					
Sardines														
Atlantic, in oil	311	20.6	24.4	0.6	354	434	3.5	510	**560**				180	
Pacific, in brine/mustard	196	18.8	12.0	1.7	303	354	5.2	**760**	260				30	
*Scallops, steamed	112	23.2	1.4	0	115	338	3.0	265	**476**					
*Shrimp	91	18.8	0.8	1.5	63	166	1.6	140	**220**	42		1.5		
Trout														
Brook	101	19.2	2.1	0	—	266								
Rainbow	195	21.5	11.4	0		—	—	—	—	—			—	—
*Tuna														
Canned in oil	288	24.2	20.5	0	6	294	1.1	**800**	301			1.0	90	
Canned in water	127	28.0	0.8	0	16	190	1.6	41	**279**					

3. EGGS

low stress

Food	Basic Food Elements				MINERALS (Milligrams)								VITAMINS	
	Food Energy Calories	Protein	Fat	Carbo-hydrates	Cal-cium	Phos-phorus	Iron	So-dium	Potas-sium	Magne-sium	Manga-nese	Zinc	Vitamin A	Vitamin C
Chicken Eggs														
whole, 1 medium	80	6	6	4	27	**205**	1.1	59	62	11		1.0	590	
Yolk	60	7	8	1	51	**205**	1.1	45	43	10.6		1.0	690	

4. MILK and DAIRY PRODUCTS

Food	Basic Food Elements				MINERALS (Milligrams)								VITAMINS	
	Food Energy Calories	Protein	Fat	Carbo-hydrates	Cal-cium	Phos-phorus	Iron	So-dium	Potas-sium	Magne-sium	Manga-nese	Zinc	Vitamin A	Vitamin C
low stress														
Buttermilk														
from skim milk	36.9	3.7	trace	4.9	121.4	95	0.04	130	**140**	14		4.0	4.1	0.8
Cheese														
American cheddar	398	25.0	32.2	2.1	**750**	478	1.0	700	82	45			1310	
Cottage, creamed	106	13.6	4.2	2.9	94	152	0.3	**229**	85				170	
Cottage, uncreamed	86	17.0	0.3	2.7	90	175	0.4	**290**	72				10	
Parmesan	393	35.7	26.1	2.9	**1142.4**	781.8	0.4	731.8	149.9	46.4			1071	
Swiss	371	27.5	27.9	1.8	**924.6**	564	1.1	710	104	43			**1449**	
Milk, skim non-instant	363	35.9	.8	52.3	1308	1016	.6	532	**1745**	143		.04	30	7
Sour cream	188	2.6	17.8	3.3	**102.3**	75.9		39.6	55.3	10			**759**	0.8
Yogurt	62	3.0	3.4	4.9	111.1	86.9		47.2	**132**				139.4	0.8
HIGH STRESS														
Butter														
salted	706	.6	81.	.4	20	16		**987**		2		0.1	**3300**	
unsalted	715	.6	82.	.4	**20**	16		8	9				**3350**	
Cheese														
American processed	370	23.2	30	1.9	697.1	478	0.9	**1136**	80	45		4.0	**1219**	
Margarine	719	0.6	80.7	0.4	20.0	16.1		985	23			0.2	**3310**	
Milk														
whole	65	3.5	3.5	4.9	117.7	92.8	0.04	49.9	**143.9**	13		0.4	143	1.1
goat's	67	3.2	4.	4.6	129	106	.1	34	**180**	17			160	1

5. VEGETABLES and VEGETABLE PRODUCTS

Food	Food Energy Calories	Basic Food Elements Protein	Fat	Carbohydrates	Calcium	Phosphorus	Iron	Sodium	Potassium	Magnesium	Manganese	Zinc	Vitamin A	Vitamin C
low stress														
Artichoke, globe	7	2.9	0.2	10.6	51	88	1.3	43	430				160	12
Asparagus, boiled	20	2.2	0.2	3.6	21	50	0.6	1	183	20			900	26
Beets, cooked	32	1.1	0.1	7.2	14	23	0.5	43	208	15			20	6
Beet Greens, raw	24	2.2	.3	4.6	119	40	3.3	130	570	106			6100	30
Broccoli, boiled	26	3.1	0.3	4.5	88	62	0.8	10	267	24			2500	90
Brussel Sprouts, boiled	36	4.2	0.4	6.4	32	72	1.1	10	273	29			520	87
Cabbage														
Chinese, raw	14	1.2	0.1	3.0	43	40	0.6	23	253	14			150	25
Headed	24	1.3	0.2	5.4	49	29	0.4	20	233	13		0.4	130	47
Red, raw	31	2.0	0.2	6.9	42	35	0.8	26	268				40	61
Carrots, raw	42	1.1	0.2	9.7	37	36	0.7	47	341	23		0.4	11,000	8
Cauliflower, boiled	22	2.3	0.2	4.1	21	42	0.7	9	206				60	55
Celery, raw	17	0.9	0.1	3.9	39	28	0.3	126	341	22	0.16		240	9
Collards, leaves, raw	45	4.8	0.8	7.5	250	82	1.5		450	57			9300	152
Corn, boiled	83	3.2	1.0	18.8	3	89	0.6		165	48		0.4	400	7
Cucumbers, with skin	15	0.9	0.1	3.4	25	27	1.1	6	160	11			250	11
Dandelion greens, raw	45	2.7	.7	9.2	187	66	3.1	76	397	36			14,000	35
Eggplant	19	1.0	.2	4.1	11	21	.6	1	150	16			10	3
Endive, raw	20	1.7	0.1	4.1	81	54	1.7	14	294	10			3300	10
Escarole, raw	20	1.7	0.1	4.1	81	54	1.7	14	294				3300	10
Garlic, raw	137	6.2	0.2	30.8	29	202	1.5	19	529					15

Food	Basic Food Elements				Minerals (Milligrams)								Vitamins	
	Food Energy Calories	Protein	Fat	Carbo-hydrates	Cal-cium	Phos-phorus	Iron	So-dium	Potas-sium	Magne-sium	Manga-nese	Zinc	Vitamin A	Vitamin C
low stress														
Kale, cooked	28	3.2	0.7	4.0	134	46	1.2	43	221	37(raw)			7400	62
Kohlrabi, raw	29	2.0	0.1	6.6	41	51	0.5	8	372	37	0.11		20	66
Lentils														
cooked	106	7.8	—	19.3	25	119	2.1	—	249				20	
raw	340	24.7	1.11	60.1	79	377	6.8	30	790	80			60	
Lettuce														
Loose leaf	18	1.3	0.3	3.5	68	25	1.4	9	264	11			1900	18
Romaine	18	1.3	0.3	3.5	68	25	1.4	9	264			0.4	1900	18
Mushrooms	28	2.7	0.3	4.4	6	116	0.8	15	414	13	0.08			3
Okra	36	2.4	0.3	7.6	92	51	0.6	3	249	41		0.28	520	31
Olives														
black	86	0.6	9.4	1.5	49.7	15	0.8	381	15.9	22			30.8	
green	185	1.0	20	3.0	105		1.5	750	25			6	40	
Onions														
dry	38	1.5	0.1	8.7	27	36	0.5	10	157	12		0.3	40	10
young green, raw	36	1.5	0.2	8.2	51	39	1.0	5	231			0.3	2000	32
Parsley	44	3.6	0.6	8.5	203	63	6.2	45	727	41	0.9		8500	172
Parsnips, raw	76	1.7	0.5	17.5	50	77	0.7	12	541	32	0.03		30	16
Peas, boiled	71	5.4	0.4	12.1	23	99	1.8	1	196	35(raw)		0.7	540	20

Food	Basic Food Elements				MINERALS (Milligrams)								VITAMINS	
	Food Energy Calories	Protein	Fat	Carbo-hydrates	Cal-cium	Phos-phorus	Iron	So-dium	Potas-sium	Magne-sium	Manga-nese	Zinc	Vitamin A	Vitamin C
Peppers														
red, raw	31	1.4	0.3	7.1	13	**30**	0.6	13					**4450**	204
sweet green, raw	22	1.2	0.2	4.8	9	22	0.7		**213**	18			420	128
Pickles, dill	11	0.7	0.2	2.2	26	21	1.0	**1428**	200	12			100	6
Radish	17	1.0	0.1	3.6	30	31	1.0	18	**322**	15			10	26
Rutabaga	46	1.1	0.1	11.0	66	39	0.4	5	**239**	15			**580**	43
Salad with raw														
lettuce	28	0.2	0.05	0.6	11.6	4.2	0.24	1.5	44	(1.9)			323	3
carrots	28	0.2	0.03	1.6	6.3	6.0	0.12	8.0	58	3.9		0.07	1870	1.4
green pepper	28	0.2	0.03	0.8	1.5	3.7	0.12	2.2	36	3.0			70	21.7
onion	28	0.3	0.02	1.5	4.6	6.0	0.08	1.7	27	2.0		0.05	7	1.7
spinach	28	0.5	0.05	0.7	15.8	8.7	0.53	12.1	80	15.0		0.14	1377	8.7
radish	28	0.2	0.02	0.6	5.0	5.2	0.17	3.0	54	2.5			2	4.3
TOTALS		1.6	0.2	5.8	44.8	33.8	1.26	28.5	**299**	28.3		0.26	**3649**	40.8
Salad with raw														
carrot	27	0.3	0.05	2.4	9.2	9.0	0.18	11.8	85.2	5.8		0.1	2750	2
celery	27	0.2	0.02	1.0	9.8	7.0	0.08	31.5	85.2	5.5			60	2.2
spinach	27	0.8	0.08	1.1	23.2	12.8	0.78	17.8	117.5	22.0		0.2	2025	12.7
tomato	27	0.3	0.05	1.2	3.2	6.8	0.12	0.8	61.0	3.5		0.05	225	5.8
TOTALS		1.6	0.2	5.7	45.4	35.6	1.16	61.9	**348.9**	36.8		0.35	**5060**	22.7

Food	Food Energy Calories	Basic Food Elements			Cal-cium	Phos-phorus	Iron	So-dium	Potas-sium	Magne-sium	Manga-nese	Zinc	Vitamin A	Vitamin C
		Protein	Fat	Carbo-hydrates										
Salad with steamed														
carrots	29	0.2	0.05	1.8	8.2	7.8	0.15	8.2	55.5			0.08	2625	1.5
green beans	29	0.4	tr.	1.4	12.6	9.2	0.15	1	37.8	8		0.08	136	3
okra	29	0.5	0.075	1.5	23	10.2	0.12	0.5	43.5	10.2			122.5	5
beets	29	0.3	0.025	1.8	3.5	5.8	0.12	10.8	52	3.8			5	1.5
TOTALS		1.4	0.15	6.5	47.3	33	0.54	20.5	188.8	22		0.16	2888.5	11
Sauerkraut	18	1.0	0.2	4.0	36	18	0.5	747	140				50	14
Soup														
Onion	26	2.2	1.05	1.9	11.5	11.5	0.2	434						
Vegetable	32	1.3	0.6	5.2	7.5	17.5	0.45	284					1264	
Squash														
Summer	19	1.1	0.1	4.2	28	29	0.4	1	202	16			410	22
Winter	50	1.4	0.3	12.4	22	38	0.6	1	369	17			3700	13
Sweet potato														
Candied	168	1.3	3.3	34.2	37	43	0.9	42	190				6300	10
Raw	114	1.7	0.4	26.3	32	47	0.7	10	243	31			8800	21
Swiss chard	25	2.4	0.3	4.6	88	39	3.2	147	550	65			6500	32
Turnips	30	1.0	0.2	6.6	39	30	0.5	49	268	20				36
Turnip greens, raw	28	3.0	.3	5.0	246	58	1.8	236	243	58			7600	139
Watercress, raw	19	2.2	.3	3.0	151	54	1.7	5.2	282	20			4900	79
Yams	101	2.1	0.2	23.2	20	69	0.6		600					9

MINERALS (Milligrams)

low stress

Food	Food Energy Calories	Basic Food Elements			MINERALS (Milligrams)								VITAMINS	
		Protein	Fat	Carbo-hydrates	Cal-cium	Phos-phorus	Iron	So-dium	Potas-sium	Magne-sium	Manga-nese	Zinc	Vitamin A	Vitamin C
Horseradish, prepared	38	1.3	0.2	9.6	61.1	32	0.9	96	290.3					1.1
Lettuce														
Butterhead	14	1.2	0.2	2.5	35	26	2.0	9	264	11			970	8
Crisphead (iceberg)	14	1.2	0.2	2.5	35	26	2.0	9	264	11	0.4		970	8
Mustard greens	31	3.0	.5	5.6	183	50	3.0	32	377	27			7000	97
Potatoes														
Baked without skin	95	2.6	0.1	21.1	9	65	0.7	4	503	22(raw)				20
French-fried	771	12.7	29.5	118.4	32	304	6.4	14	2,295					41
Mashed	340	7.7	.5	77.6	73	177	3.2	358	1,039				140	29
Spinach	26	3.2	0.3	4.3	93	51	3.1	71	470	88	0.8		8100	51
Spinach, New Zealand	19	2.2	.3	3.1	58	46	2.6	159	795	166	1.6		4300	30
Tomatoes	22	1.1	0.2	4.7	13	27	0.5	3	244	14	0.2		900	23
Tomato catsup	106	2.0	0.4	25.4	22	50	0.8	1042	363	21			1400	15
Tomato paste	82	3.4	0.4	18.6	27	70	3.5	38	888	20			3300	49
Tomato puree	39	1.7	0.2	8.9	13	34	1.7	399	426	20			1600	3.3

6. DRY BEANS, PEAS and NUTS

Food	Food Energy Calories	Basic Food Elements			Cal-cium	Phos-phorus	MINERALS (Milligrams)			Magne-sium	Manga-nese	Zinc	VITAMINS	
		Protein	Fat	Carbo-hydrates			Iron	So-dium	Potas-sium				Vitamin A	Vitamin C

(low stress)

Beans

Lima, cooked	138	8.2	0.6	25.6	29	154	3.1	2	612					
Mung, sprouted, cooked	28	3.2	tr.	5.6	16.8	48	0.88	4	156			0.9	24	6.4
Pinto, dry	349	22.9	1.2	63.7	135	457	6.4	10	984					
Snap green, cooked	24	1.6	tr.	5.6	50.4	37	0.6	4	151	32		0.3	544	12

Lentils

| cooked | 106 | 7.8 | 0 | 19.3 | 25 | 119 | 2.1 | — | 249 | | | | 20 | |
| raw | 340 | 24.7 | 1.1 | 60.1 | 79 | 377 | 6.8 | 30 | 790 | 80 | | | 60 | |

Food	Basic Food Elements				MINERALS (Milligrams)								VITAMINS	
	Food Energy Calories	Protein	Fat	Carbo-hydrates	Cal-cium	Phos-phorus	Iron	So-dium	Potas-sium	Magne-sium	Manga-nese	Zinc	Vitamin A	Vitamin C
HIGH STRESS														
Nuts														
Almonds	598	18.6	54.2	19.5	234	504	4.7	4	**773**	270				
Peanuts, boiled	564	26.0	47.5	18.6	69	401	2.1	5	**674**	206				
Pinole	635	13.0	60.5	20.5	12	**604**	5.2						30	
Nuts														
Brazil	646	14.4	65.9	11.0	186	**693**	**6.8**	1	670	225				10
Butternuts	629	23.7	61.2	8.4	—	—		—	—	—				
Cashew	561	17.2	45.7	29.3	38	373	3.8	15	**464**	267			100	
Chestnuts	191	2.8	1.5	41.5	29	87	1.7	2	**410**					
Filberts (hazelnuts)	647	10.7	63.3	20	253	320	3.3	0.7	**473**				106.7	7.3
Hickory nuts	673	14	67.3	13.3	—	—	**2.7**	—	—	—				
Macadamia	692	7.8	71.7	15.9	48.1	161.1	2.0	—	**264**	—				
Peanuts														
raw	565	25.9	47.4	18.6	69.1	400.2	2.1	5.1	**674.7**	175				
roasted, salted	586	26.0	49.7	18.8	74.2	401.5	2.1	418.4	**674.7**	175				
roasted, unsalted	581	26.2	48.8	20.6	71.9	407.4	2.2	5.1	**699.6**	175		3.0		
Pecans	688	9.2	71.3	14.6	73.1	289.3	2.4		**603.6**	142			130.2	1.5
Pistachio	594	19.3	53.8	19.0	131.1	500.5	7.3	—	**973**	—			229.6	
Walnuts, black	628	20.7	59.6	15.1	—	**570**	6.0	3	460	190			302	
Walnuts, english	654	15.0	64.4	15.6	83	380	2.1	2	**450**	131			30	3
Soybeans	403	34.1	17.7	33.5	226	554	8.4	5	**1677**	265			80	

7. FRUIT and FRUIT PRODUCTS

Food	Food Energy Calories	Basic Food Elements			Calcium	Phosphorus	MINERALS (Milligrams)						VITAMINS	
		Protein	Fat	Carbohydrates			Iron	Sodium	Potassium	Magnesium	Manganese	Zinc	Vitamin A	Vitamin C
low stress														
Acerola cherry, raw	28	.4	.3	6.8	12	11	.2	8	83					1300
Apple, raw unpared	58	0.2	0.6	14.5	7	10	0.3	1	110	8	.04	.1	90	4
Apricots														
dried, uncooked	260	5.0	0.5	66.5	67	108	5.5	26	979	45			10,900	12
raw	51	1.0	0.2	12.8	17	23	.5	1	281	12			2700	10
Avocado	167	2.1	16.4	6.3	10	42	0.6	3	604				290	14
Blackberries	58	1.2	0.9	12.9	32	19	0.9	1	170	30	0.59		200	21
Blueberries	62	0.7	0.5	15.3	15	13	1.0	1	81	10	3.4		100	14
Cantaloupe	30	0.7	0.1	7.5	14	16	0.4	12	251	16			3400	33
Cherries, sweet	70	1.3	0.3	17.4	22	19	0.4	2	191				110	
Coconut, fresh meat	346	3.5	35.3	9.4	13	95	1.7	23	256	46				3
Currants, red or white	50	1.4	0.2	12.1	32	23	1.0	2	257				120	41
Dates, dry, pitted	274	2.2	0.5	72.9	59	63	3.0	1	648	58			50	
Elderberries	72	2.6	(0.5)	16.4	38	28	1.6	—	300	—			600	36
Figs														
dried	274	4.3	1.3	69.1	126	77	3.0	34	640	71			80	
raw	80	1.2	0.3	20.3	35	22	0.6	2	194	20			80	2
Grapes														
American	69	1.3	1.0	15.7	16	12	0.4	3	158	13			100	4
European	67	0.6	0.3	17.3	12	20	0.4	3	173	6			100	4
Honeydew	33	0.8	0.3	7.7	14	16	0.4	12	251				40	23
Mangos	66	.7	.4	16.8	10	13	.4	7	189	18			4800	35

Food	Basic Food Elements				Minerals (Milligrams)								Vitamins	
	Food Energy Calories	Protein	Fat	Carbo-hydrates	Cal-cium	Phos-phorus	Iron	So-dium	Potas-sium	Magne-sium	Manga-nese	Ainc	Vitamin A	Vitamin C
Nectarines	64	.6		17.1	4	24	.5	6	294	13			1650	13
Papayas	39	.6	.1	10.	20	16	.3	3	234				1750	56
Peaches														
dried	262	3.1	0.7	68.3	48	117	6.0	16	950	10	0.11	0.2	3900	18
raw	38	0.6	0.1	9.7	9	19	0.5	1	202				1330	7
Pears														
dried	126	1.5	0.8	31.7	16	23	0.6	3	269	5	0.06	0.16	30	2
raw	61	0.7	0.4	15.3	8	11	0.3	2	130				20	4
Prunes	75	0.8	0.2	19.7	12	18	0.5	1	170	40			300	4
Pumpkin	26	1.0	0.1	6.5	21	44	0.8	1	340	12			1600	9
Raisins	289	2.5	0.2	77.4	62	101	3.5	27	763	35			20	1
Raspberries														
black	73	1.5	1.4	15.7	30	22	0.9	1	199					18
red	57	1.2	0.5	13.6	22	22	0.9	1	168				130	25
Strawberries	37	0.7	0.5	8.4	21	21	1.0	1	164	12	0.06		60	59
Watermelon	26	0.5	0.2	6.4	7	10	0.5	1	100	8			590	7
HIGH STRESS														
Bananas	85	1.1	0.2	22.2	8	26	0.7	1	370	33		0.2	190	10
Cherries, sour	58	1.2	0.3	14.3	22	19	0.4	2	191				1000	10
Grapefruit	41	0.5	0.09	10.6	16.2	16.2	0.4	0.9	135				81.1	37.8
Limes	28	0.7	0.2	9.5	33	18	0.6	2	102				10	37
Oranges	49	1.0	0.2	12.2	41	20	0.4	1	200	11	0.03	0.17	200	50
Pineapple	52	0.4	0.2	13.7	17	8	0.5	1	146	13			70	17

8. CEREAL GRAINS and GRAIN PRODUCTS

Food	Food Energy Calories	Basic Food Elements			Cal-cium	Phos-phorus	MINERALS (Milligrams)						VITAMINS	
		Protein	Fat	Carbo-hydrates			Iron	So-dium	Potas-sium	Magne-sium	Manga-nese	Zinc	Vitamin A	Vitamin C
low stress														
Barley, pearled	350	8	1	79	16	**189**	2.0	3	160	37				
Bread, whole wheat	240	12	4	48	100	228	3.2	**527**	273	78		1.8		
Buckwheat, dark flour	333	11.7	2.5	72.0	33	347	2.8	1	**656**					
Buckwheat, light flour	347	6.4	1.2	79.5	11	88	1.0	1	**320**					
Carob flour	180	4.5	1.4	80.7	**352**	81								
Millet	325	9.8	2.9	72.4	20		6.7		**427**					
Oatmeal	390	14.25	7.4	68.2	52.5	**405**	4.5	2	327.5	144		3.4		
Rye Wafers	346	15.4	tr.	77	53.9	388	3.8	**882**	600					
Wheat bran	213	16.0	4.6	61.9	119	**1276**	14.9	9	1121	490		9.8		
Wheat germ	360	27	11	47	70	**1118**	9.0	3	827	336		14.3		
Wheat shredded	360	8	4	80	44	**388**	3.6	3	348	133		2.8		
HIGH STRESS														
Crackers														
graham	385	8.0	9.4	73.4	40	149	1.5	**671**	385	51		1.1		
saltines	434	9.0	12	71.6	21	90	1.2	**1102**	120			0.5		
soda	440	9.2	13.1	70.7	22	89	1.5	**1100**	120	29				
whole wheat	404	8.4	13.8	68.3	23	190	0.3	**548**	190					
Macaroni	370	12.5	1.2	75.0	26.8	161.7	1.3	2.0	**196.7**	48		1.5		
Yeast, baker's compressed	86	12.1	0.4	11.0	13.0	394	4.9	16.1	**610.8**	59				

9. FATS and OILS

Food	Basic Food Elements				MINERALS (Milligrams)								VITAMINS	
	Food Energy Calories	Protein	Fat	Carbo-hydrates	Cal-cium	Phos-phorus	Iron	So-dium	Potas-sium	Magne-sium	Manga-nese	Zinc	Vitamin A	Vitamin C
HIGH STRESS														
Cornstarch	362	0.31	trace	87.7	0	0	0	trace	trace	0			0	0
Cottonseed oil	885	0	100	0	0	0	0.5	0	0	0		0	0	0
Gravy, meat, brown	205	1.5	17.5	10.0	trace			*	10					
Mayonnaise	721	1.1	80.0	2.1	21.4	28.6	0.07	599	35.7				278	
Mustard, yellow, prepared	75	4.7	4.4	6.4	83.8	72.8	2.0	1250	129.8					
Shortening, vegetable	879	—	98.6	—	0	0	0	—	—	48		0	0	0

* = Sodium content is largely dependent upon salt added in preparation and cooking

10. SUGARS, SWEETS and SYRUPS

Food	Basic Food Elements				MINERALS (Milligrams)								VITAMINS	
	Food Energy Calories	Protein	Fat	Carbo-hydrates	Cal-cium	Phos-phorus	Iron	So-dium	Potas-sium	Magne-sium	Manga-nese	Zinc	Vitamin A	Vitamin C
HIGH STRESS														
Cane syrup	284	0.5	0.2	72.6	70	42	1.2		445					3
Honey, strained	306	0.2	0	78.0	20	16	0.8	5	51	3				
Maple syrup	250	0	0	64.0	165	15	1.0	15	130					1
Molasses, Blackstrap	27			6.8	85	10	2	12	365	32				
Sorghum syrup	260			13.4	30	5	2.4	4	120					

11. FOOD JUICES, BEVERAGES

Food	Basic Food Elements				Minerals (Milligrams)								Vitamins	
	Food Energy Calories	Protein	Fat	Carbohydrates	Calcium	Phosphorus	Iron	Sodium	Potassium	Magnesium	Manganese	Zinc	Vitamin A	Vitamin C

low stress

Food Juices

Food	Food Energy Calories	Protein	Fat	Carbohydrates	Calcium	Phosphorus	Iron	Sodium	Potassium	Magnesium	Manganese	Zinc	Vitamin A	Vitamin C
Acerola	23	.4	.3	4.8	**10**	9	.5	3	**101**	4		.05		**1600**
Apple	47	.1		11.9	6	9	.6	1						1
Carrot	42	1.1	0.2	9.7	37	36	0.7	47	**341**	23	0.16	0.4	**11,000**	8
Celery	17	0.9	0.1	3.9	39	28	0.3	126	**341**	22			240	9
Grape	66	0.2	trace	16.6	11	12	0.3	2	**116**	12				
Pear/Carrot														
Pear	52	0.4	0.2	7.6	4	5.5	0.2	1	65	2.5	0.03	0.08	10	2
Carrot	52	0.6	0.1	4.8	18.5	18	0.4	23.5	170	11.5		0.2	5500	4
TOTALS		**1.0**	**0.3**	**12.4**	**22.5**	**23.5**	**0.6**	**24.5**	**235**	**14.0**	**0.03**	**0.28**	**5510**	**6**
Pear/Celery														
Pear	39	0.4	0.2	7.6	4	5.5	0.2	1	65	2.5	0.03	0.08	10	2
Celery	39	0.5	0.05	1.9	19.5	14	0.15	63	170	11	0.08		120	4.5
TOTALS		**0.9**	**0.25**	**9.5**	**23.5**	**19.5**	**0.35**	**64**	**235**	**13.5**	**0.11**	**0.08**	**130**	**6.5**

HIGH STRESS

Food	Food Energy Calories	Protein	Fat	Carbohydrates	Calcium	Phosphorus	Iron	Sodium	Potassium	Magnesium	Manganese	Zinc	Vitamin A	Vitamin C
Coffee, instant	98.1	trace	trace	trace	2	4	.1	1	**36**					
Food Juices														
Orange	**45**	.4	**.2**	**10.2**	**11**	**17**	**.2**	1	**200**	11		.02	200	50
Pineapple, unsweetened	55	.4	.1	13.5	15	9	.3	1	149	12			50	9
Tomato juice canned	19	.9	.1	4.3	7	18	.9	200	227	10			**800**	16

SCRIPTURE VERSE at the top of
each page to guide you through
the day.

QUESTIONS ANSWERED
Over 50 of the most commonly
asked questions about the
Reams program and nutrition
in general! Concise, clear
answers that are easy to follow.

PLANNING IN ADVANCE
Tells you what to
have on hand for
the next two days
of your better-health
diet plan.

AUNT EFFIE'S REMEDIES
You'll laugh at Aunt Effie
as she comes up with some
old fashioned remedies
for common ailments!

PLUS much, more more...

3-Day TURN-AROUND DIET
Reams Recommendations
Special health recipes

Bless the Lord, O my soul, and forget not all
His benefits: Who forgiveth all thine iniquities;
Who healeth all thy diseases . . . *Psalm 103:1-3*

WEEK **1** DAY **1**

MONDAY

QUESTIONS FREQUENTLY ASKED . . .

**Why Breakfast, Dinner, Supper?
Shouldn't the big meal be at night?**

Most people have been conditioned to
Breakfast, Lunch and Dinner . . . eating
their biggest meal in the evening. This
is wrong! A large meal eaten in the
evening ~~is~~ st
of illr
Luncl   WELL-PLANNED
a sut   MENUS
time, y   Based on
it off a   nutrition
eat a la   guidelines
do you   suggested by
And pro   Dr. Carey Reams!
You will
Breakfast—Dinner—Supper plan with
hearty meals designed for breakfast
and mid-day. That's why we call it
Breakfast, **Dinner** and Supper.

**AUNT EFFIE . . .
Have you seen Cora Mae's Shingles?**

No, but the rest of her house is a mess!
Oughta have her body chemistry
checked, first-off. I tried a "triple-
header" when I had them. First, took
daily a vitamin-mineral supplement.
Then, rubbed Vitamin E oil on the
Shingles. And then alternated with
Lemon water applied liberally. It
worked!

BREAKFAST

1 fruit   1/2 grapefruit
1 toast
Hot herb tea or coffee
Hot shredded wheat cooked in
   skim milk
   Soak in skim milk over night.
Milk

DINNER

Fresh vegetable salad
Cornbread
Cup of vegetable broth
Vegetable scallops with mush-
   rooms and garden peas

SUPPER

Leafy vegetable salad
1 slice of whole wheat toast
Hot herb tea or milk
Soup du jour
1 yogurt

LOOKING AHEAD

Tuesday
Soak grits overnight tonight. Buy
vegetarian breakfast sausage and
chicken, asparagus, corn,
squash, graham crackers, apple
juice.
Wednesday
Buy oranges, oatmeal, salad
items, chow mein, rice, cranberry
juice, yogurt, bananas, meatless
Irish stew, and molasses cookies.

WHAT! ME FAST?
YOU MUST BE CRAZY?
I'D DIE OF STARVATION!
I COULDN'T EXIST IF I MISSED ONE
MEAL!

(If reading a book on fasting
causes a reaction
like the young lady pictured
then
THIS BOOK IS FOR YOU!
I dare you to read it!
It can change your life
    for the better!

Fasting is **not** starving. And short, periodic fasts may start you on the road to
better health and a longer and happier
life!)

NATURE'S OLDEST REMEDY ... <u>FASTING</u> ... CAN MAKE YOU ALIVE AGAIN!

HOW TO KEEP
HEALTHY & HAPPY
BY FASTING
by Salem Kirban

• Can fasting relieve tension? • Will fasting help me to sleep better? • Can fasting eliminate that "dragged out" feeling upon awakening? • Can fasting lower cholesterol levels? • Can I lose weight quickly and easily by fasting? • Can fasting end my dependence on smoking and drinking? • How fasting can slow your aging process and improve your marriage!

Charts and Photographs!

1 **GO WITHOUT FOOD? PERISH THE THOUGHT!**
Americans are Food Oriented • Tell Me What You Eat and I'll Tell You What You Are • Specialists and Physicians • The Value of Rest • Health is Wealth

2 **FESTIVALS OF FEASTING**
A dinner of 40 Courses • Canary a la King • The $40,000 Dinner • A Law Limiting Food Purchases • The Bible on Gluttony • Jeroboam's Counterfeit Feast • The Feast Where Salome Danced • Proper Occasions for Feasting

3 **MUNCHIES, CRUNCHIES and FRENCH FRIES**
Don't Steam the Roll • An Average American Diet • The All-American Lunch • The Sickly Supper • Seduction by TV • $250,000 for One Minute • Take White Bread • Take Breakfast Cereals • Synthetic Vitamins ... a Bait • Ice Cream Isn't Nice Cream • Foods I Avoid

4 **HOW'S YOUR LIVER, LATELY?**
Your Life is in Your Liver • Functions of Food Additives • No Wonder We Get Sick • The Curse of Indirect Additives (or More Poisons At No Added Cost) • Conversation of Tomorrow • The "Miracle" Additives • Chinese Syndrome • Show Me Your Liver and I'll Show You Your Life!

5 **DANIEL HAD A BETTER WAY**
Daniel's Diet Gave Him 2 Kingdoms • Daniel Refused the King's Food • The Vegetable Diet • Daniel Had a Better Idea • The Results of the 10-day Test • Nebuchadnezzar's Reaction • Daniel's Wisdom Should be Ours • Give Up Those Junk Foods and Start Living • Don't Expect a Miracle Overnight

6 **YOU MEAN HIPPOCRATES FASTED**
Diet Rather Than Drugs • Nature ... The Principal Healer • Famous Fasters • The Paradox of Hospitals • Prevention Instead of Treatment

7 **DOES THE BIBLE APPROVE OF FASTING?**
Daniel Fasted 3 Weeks • 8 Occasions for Fasting • Does the Bible Approve • 5 Guidelines When Fasting

8 **GIVE ME 7 GOOD REASONS FOR FASTING**
What is Fasting • Fasting Clinics • How Does the Fasting Process Work • Your Miracle Kidneys • The Value of Water • Fasting Eliminates Toxins • The Royal Road to Healing • Fasting Saves Time • 3 Hours Saved • Fasting and Arthritis • Fasting and the Peptic Ulcer • Fasting and Hay Fever • Fasting and the Heart • Fasting and Colitis • Fasting and the Prostate Gland •

9 **CAN I LOSE WEIGHT BY FASTING?**
Two Causes • Dangers in Being Overweight • 5 Pounds in One Day • High in Protein • High in Carbohydrates • Saturated Fats • Unsaturated Fats • Consistency Needed • How Fast Can I Lose Weight by Fasting • Some Good Advice

10 **WILL FASTING LOWER MY BLOOD PRESSURE?**
A Symptom ... Not a Disease • Drugs May Produce Adverse Effects • We Live in a *STRESS* Environment • Warning Signs • An Ounce of Prevention • How's Your Arterial Resiliency • Fasting is Scriptural

11 **HOW DO I BEGIN FASTING?**
Witch Doctors Frighten Disease • The Doctor's Helpers • Illness Costs Sky Rocket • How to Save Time and Money • Psychosomatic Illnesses • Those Who Should Not Fast • Fasting Works • How to Succeed in Fasting

12 **The 24-HOUR FAST**
Fasting is Not Starving • Your Body Will Signal You • When Should I Begin My Fast • Drink Only Water • Distilled vs. Mineral Water • But Won't I Feel Hungry • What to Expect • My Personal Experience • You Will Not Feel Hungry

13 **HOW TO BREAK THE 24-HOUR FAST**
Inside Your Intestines • When the Villi Become Villains • 3500 Villi Per Square Inch • A Coated Tongue • How to Break Your Fast • The Day Your Tastebuds Come Alive • Let's Look at Your Tastebuds • Do You Realize What You Are Doing • Why Did I Say All That • Forget Animal Products • Your Second Meal

14 **HOW LONG SHOULD I FAST**
One Man's Fasting Schedule • Elimination Diminishes • A Nutritious Meal • The Word is Spreading • Put a Spring Back in Your Step • Shun Cakes and Creams • Turn Duty into Joy

---

"QUOTES"

You will not feel hungry when you fast! I know ... because I have tried it. Not only will you NOT feel hungry ... but for once in your life ... you will feel **ALIVE!**

* * *

HOW TO KEEP HEALTHY & HAPPY BY FASTING $2.95

SAMPLE PAGE from
HOW TO KEEP HEALTHY and HAPPY BY FASTING

**Americans
are
Food-oriented**

Americans have been so bombarded with television commercials from fast-food drive-ins . . that to think for one minute of skipping a meal almost borders on being unpatriotic!

We are food-oriented. And we actually believe that it is necessary for us to have 3 square meals a day. We pride ourself on having fat babies and wouldn't think of skipping breakfast!

We are so grateful that we live in the land of Shake 'n Bake bags and can cook our food in sturdy plastic containers.

Everything we seem to do in America is ON THE RUN. We eat on the run . . . and die on the run.

Our economy and much of our advertising is based on the fact that happiness can only come from material success in life . . . those extra accessories on the car . . . the ability to "have it your way" when ordering your fat-saturated hamburger . . . the thrill of "smoking for taste and not for tar."

In this book, I may repeat myself on this one particular point . . . because many people find it difficult to understand.

**YOU WILL NOT
FEEL HUNGRY
WHEN YOU FAST!**

I know . . . because I have tried it; as have countless thousands. Not only will you NOT feel hungry . . . but for once in your life . . . you will feel ALIVE!

**Health
is
Wealth**

During the depression of the 1930's my family was on welfare. As a lad of 8 and 9, we grew a garden and had to eat unpreserved foods from it. We could not afford candy bars. Instead we would chew on a rhubarb or a carrot.

And believe it or not . . . we had no TV. It hadn't been invented yet! So for enjoyment . . . my mother and sister and I would rock on the swing that we hung between two trees — the world's best tranquilizer.

And my mother, in her broken Lebanese-English accent, would say,

Son, HEALTH IS WEALTH

How true that is!

Health is a crown on a well man's head, but no one can see it but a sick man.

How is your crown? Is it frayed, tarnished and starting to fall apart? Don't depend on your doctor to put it back together again. Go without food? Perish the thought!

**The
CHOICE
IS
YOURS**

Just this once . . . learn how going without food on a fast . . . may start you down a road of health and happiness you never thought possible!

Go back to stuffing yourself at every meal . . . getting up from the table bloated and sleepy. You have the choice to make.

Wake up every morning feeling dull and dragged out and more tired than when you went to bed.

Go spend money at your doctor's office and come out with a prescription and take myriad variety of pills.

**NOW! SIMPLY, CLEARLY WITHOUT ANY PHYSICAL EXAMINATION
A Urine/Saliva TEST CAN ACCURATELY DETERMINE YOUR PRESENT
AND FUTURE HEALTH PROBLEMS according to Dr. Carey Reams!**

HEALTH GUIDE FOR SURVIVAL
by Salem Kirban

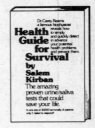

> The book that tells why Dr. Carey Reams believes Heart
> Attacks can be foreseen from minutes, to months, to years in
> advance—and prevented! • Breast Cancer can be avoided! •
> Leukemia is one of the easiest things to correct! • Hyperten-
> sion can be corrected quickly without tranquilizers!

High in the mountains of Georgia, down a 2½ mile dirt road, lived an unassuming, humble biophysicist, Dr. Carey Reams. People from all over the world beat a path to his door...although there are no signs to indicate where he lives!

Why? Because Dr. Reams has an impressive track record of saving those who medical doctors have given up all hope on and pronounced "terminally ill." Dr. Reams is NOT a medical doctor, nor does he diagnose or treat disease.

How? Through a simple, ingenious urine/saliva test. Dr. Reams is a mathematical genius. This test gives him the proper information to mathematically analyze the entire body chemistry and detect, with remarkable accuracy, both the location and severity of most physical ailments. With a unique 3-day fast and special lemon-water, distilled water diet, Dr. Reams is able to restore body chemistry to its normal range and suggest a diet for an individual's specific body chemistry.

Truth is stranger than fiction! Cancer, heart trouble, arthritis, diabetes, hypertension, leukemia, hypoglycemia, breast cancer, glaucoma, multiple sclerosis, emphysema and even leprosy—people with all these diseases and many more have passed through Dr. Reams' retreat and responded to an individualized diet!

To your loved ones and friends who are terminally ill or have a serious disease... you owe it to them to at least read **HEALTH GUIDE FOR SURVIVAL.** It may prove the key that will return them to perfect health and a long, full useful life!

Revealing Quotes from Health Guide for Survival

The doctor may pronounce you in perfect health. You can feel well and yet be in imminent danger of a fatal heart attack!

We welcome a challenge...whenever one takes enough time and interest to make the tests, we have never been wrong!

I do not claim to have a cure of any kind. We make no claims of any kind. We make tests and using the mathematics of body and food chemistry, compute a diet that can bring the body back towards the mathematical formula for perfect health. Whatever healing takes place is done by God and the life forces in the body.

In one two-year period alone I tested and designed nutritional programs for over 24,000 people. Over 10,000 of these people were given up to die.

There is *one single mineral* that is of the greatest benefit in the *prevention of breast cancer!*
Vitamins are only a crutch. They can aggravate your problems.

People have come here bedfast by *arthritis* and drive away in their own car three weeks later.

I am the advisor now on diet for many, many medical doctors. I am an ordained minister teaching the health message as written in the Bible.

Cobalt cooks the flesh. *Chemotheraphy* destroys the liver.

Hypertension in children and adults can be corrected quickly without the use of tranquilizers!

Gall bladder problems in the early stages are very easy to solve.

We have had children come here with leukemia and we have had 100% success! *Leukemia* is one of the easiest things to correct!

If you follow the rules of good health your *weight* will stay where it is supposed to be. Weight clubs treat every person as though they are obese, and they are not!

HEALTH GUIDE FOR SURVIVAL $3.95

BOOKS on Health by PAUL C. BRAGG

Paul C. Bragg was himself the best testimonial for the value of his teachings. His books are read by thousands around the world, and his teachings are followed by famous people such as Billy Graham, Doris Day, Conrad Hilton and Jack LaLane. Gloria Swanson was one of his first health students. Paul Bragg was a physical therapist and a giant in the field of nutrition, health and physical fitness. For over 40 years he counselled Kings, Queens, Politicians, Sportsmen and Statesmen. As a result of a near drowning accident in Hawaii, he died suddenly on December 5, 1976 at 95.

THE MIRACLE OF FASTING
by Paul C. Bragg
Single copy: $3.95
In 33 inspiring chapters, Paul Bragg reveals new discoveries about an old miracle for agelessness, physical, mental and spiritual rejuvenation. Interesting highlights include his own experiences in fasting.

HOW TO KEEP YOUR HEART HEALTHY AND FIT
by Paul C. Bragg
Single copy: $2.95
Are you a candidate for a heart attack? Learn how to fight this No. 1 killer! You will find this book a guide to the prevention and control of heart problems. Well worth the price!

PREPARING FOR MOTHERHOOD NATURE'S WAY
by Paul C. Bragg
Single copy: $2.95
An excellent guidebook for the mother-to-be and for the mother. You will find everything from proper prenatal exercises to proper nutrition for your baby and for you. A must for every mother!

GOLDEN KEYS TO INTERNAL PHYSICAL FITNESS
by Paul C. Bragg
Single copy: $2.95
This book tells you how to live long, stay healthy and be youthful! Life can begin (or end) at 40. If you are starting to feel sluggish at 40, 50 or 60, this book will reveal how you can be internally fit!

NATURE'S HEALING SYSTEM FOR BETTER EYESIGHT REGARDLESS OF AGE
Single copy: $2.95
This book will open your eyes to better vision. It will show you how your eyes can heal themselves and how to keep your eyes sparkling and youthful. Quick, easy steps!

HEALTH FOOD COOKBOOK
by Paul C. Bragg
Single copy: $4.95
Here you will find 1000 of the world's finest health recipes! Recipes to supercharge your body with youthful vitality and longevity! Plus Herb Charts, Vitamin-Mineral Charts and Weight Control Menus.

Prices on above books include postage and packing.

SPECIAL ANNIVERSARY SALE!

(Minimum Order for 20% discount is $10)

20% OFF
EVERYTHING

Not only are we giving you 20% off *everything* in this catalog, but you also get these EXTRA GIFTS as a BONUS!

FREE with any order of $10 or more...
    1.   Sample copy TOTAL HEALTH GUIDE NEWSLETTER

PLUS these <u>*added*</u> *Gifts for an order of $25 or more...*
    1.   Vitamin Pocket-Pack (holds full day's supply)
    2.   Calorie Wheel (count your daily calories)

Plus these <u>*added*</u> *Gifts for an order of $100 or more...*

Sankyo 400
CONTEMPORARY DIGITAL CLOCK

  * Extremely quiet electric operation
  * Easy to read amber numerals
  * Compact design, built-to-last
  * Digital Hour, Minute and Seconds

Palmtronic 8S
Canon Calculator

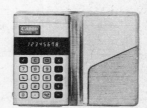

  * 8-digit fluorescent display
  * Automatic constant/4-arithmetic functions
  * Percent key for percentage calculations
  * Full-floating decimal system
  * Handy size: 2 3/4" x 4 5/8" x 7/16"

Salem Kirban Family Catalog Order Form

Salem Kirban, Inc.
Kent Road, Huntingdon Valley, Penna. 19006

Please Print

Mr./Mrs./Miss _____

Address _____

City _____ State _____ Zip _____

Name of Item	Qty.	Price Each	Total Price
		TOTAL	$
	20% Discount		
		Add PACKING charge	1.00
		TOTAL PAYMENT enclosed	$

SHARE YOUR HAPPINESS WITH A FRIEND

Do you have friends or relatives who are interested in nutrition and gifts that uplift and bring joy? Let us send them a 1-year subscription to our FAMILY CATALOG **free!** Just print their names and addresses below.

Mr.
Miss
Mrs. _____

Mr.
Miss
Mrs. _____

Address _____

Address _____

City _____ State _____ ZIP _____

City _____ State _____ ZIP _____

100% GUARANTEE! When you buy from us...you become a part of our family. We will give you a full refund on every item returned unused!